COWBOY BEBOP

Vol.006

Anime Guide

TOKYOPOP

WE GOT THE JAZZ.

COWBOY BEBOP Characters

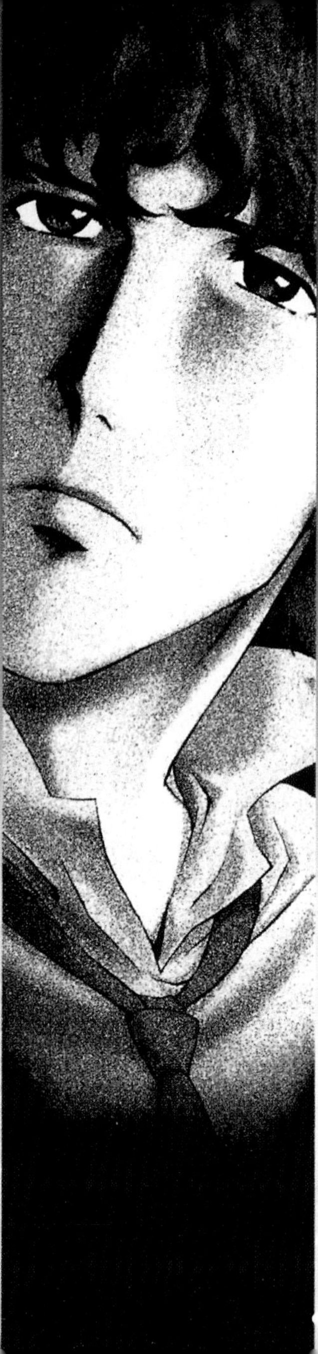

SPIKE SPIEGEL

The protagonist of our story. A 27 year old bounty hunter who loves to live free. Until three years ago he was a member of the Red Dragon syndicate, and along with his friend, Vicious, showed great promise for becoming one of the leaders in the organization. But the friendship crumbled when Spike fell in love with Julia, Vicious' lover. Spike faked his death and left the syndicate, resolved never to see Julia or Vicious again, fading into the dark recesses of society by becoming a bounty hunter. His past is more like a dream to him than a collection of memories, a seemingly endless dream from which he'll never awaken. But the dream will end soon, and Spike's past will become more real than he ever imagined. When angels are cast out of Heaven, they become devils. Can an angel that has been cast from Heaven, possibly return to Heaven?

JET BLACK

A bounty hunter, and Spike's partner. A 36 year old ex-cop. The owner of the Bebop, which serves not only as their home and transportation, but also their office, their recreation center, and even a hostel at times. Ever since Jet teamed up with Spike three years ago, their relationship has been tested time and time again, but the bond of mutual trust between them has never been broken. They both suffer from unhealed emotional wounds, and understand the unyielding pain of loss. And so they offer each other a tacit compassion and invaluable companionship. Notice the kindness he shows to Spike in the final episode. He's naturally kind, that guy Jet.

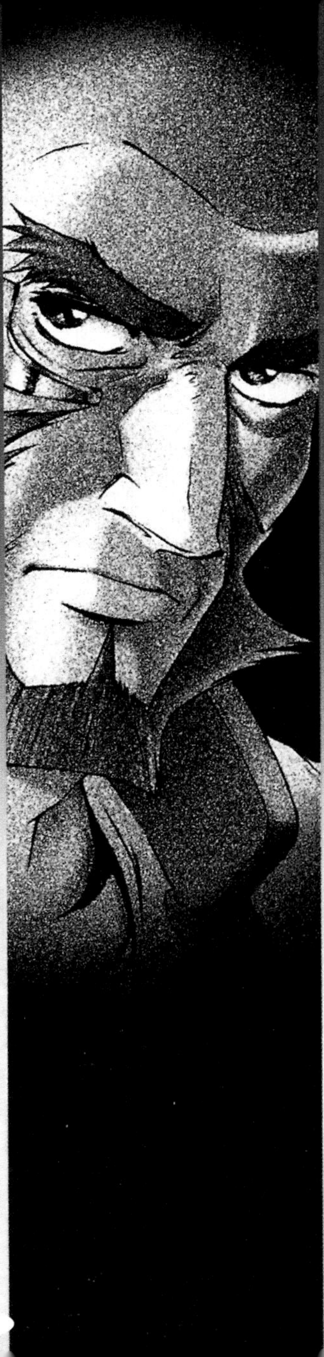

COWBOY BEBOP Characters

COWBOY BEBOP Characters

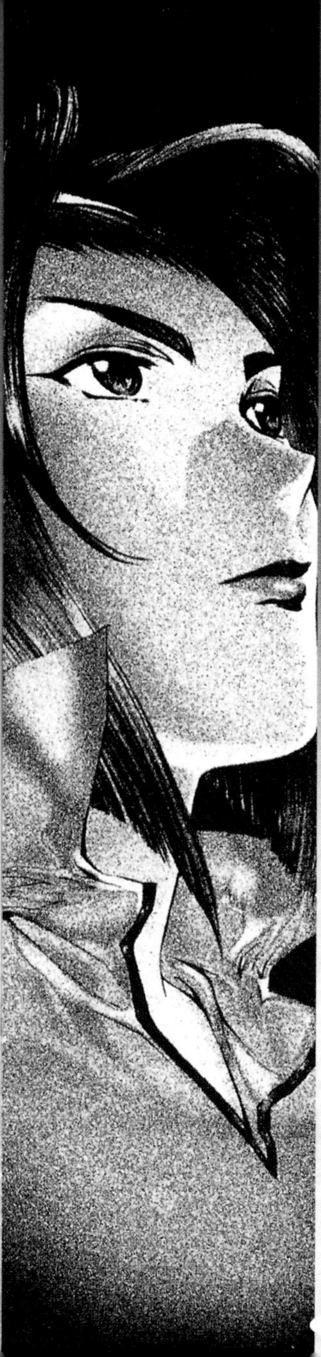

FAYE VALENTINE

A female bounty hunter who burrowed her way into the Bebop in episode three. When she woke up from a 54-year cold sleep three years ago, she found herself shouldering a huge debt from the procedure, though she can't remember ever authorizing cryogenic freezing. Actually, all of her memories are gone, her past, her identity, even her real name. She sought to regain those memories, but the few she did recover left such a bitter residue that she preferred not to know, building a new life for herself with the Bebop and its crew. But in the three years she's been out of hibernation, she's added to her financial burden by racking up a heavy gambling debt.

ED & EIN

Edward Wong Hau Pepelu Tivrusky IV (or Ed for short). She was once an orphan living on earth, but when she found out about the Bebop on the computer network, she decided to join Spike and the others. Her father appears in Session 24, and it's revealed that this superhuman character really takes after her father. When she is reunited with her father, a big change comes over her......

The Welsh Corgi Ein, a data dog with a deceivingly high intelligence. He arrives aboard the Bebop under unusual circumstances, and leaves the Bebop under even more unusual circumstances.

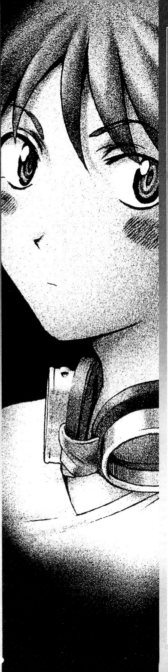
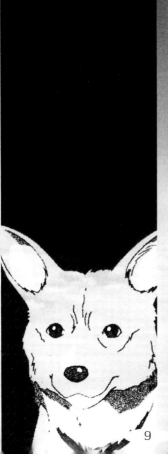

VICIOUS

A radical-wing lieutenant within the Red Dragon syndicate. Age 27. Once had a strong fraternal kinship with Spike, but ever since Spike left the syndicate, their relationship has been hostile and fraught with hatred. No one knows if the hostility between them is born out of Vicious' dedication to the code of the syndicate, or because he feels Spike seduced Julia. Only one thing is for sure - he doesn't care how much blood he spills in his quest to kill Spike. For him, the only thing that can pacify his rage... is death.

JULIA

Disappeared and went into hiding three years ago. To Vicious, she is an ex-lover; to Spike, she is a soul mate untimely ripped from him by wicked circumstance. Up until now, she has only appeared in flashback sequences and, briefly, in images during the ending theme of the show, but in the final session, she finally shows herself. She's been living on the run from the Red Dragons (who are chasing her, most likely at Vicious' instigation). Recently Lin's brother Shin (both of whom knew Spike from his days with the syndicate) told her about the shift of power within the Red Dragons, and gave her information about Spike and the others.

Hard Lu

This episode, the penultimate story in this series, at long last reveals tangible morsels of Faye and Ed's respective pasts. Prompted by a video that her past self had sent to her, Faye visits the place where she may very well have lived, and happens upon an old friend. Meanwhile, Ed stops by the convent in which she used to live as an orphan, and learns about her real father. Are these unexpected events a turn for the better or a turn for the worse for the girls of the Bebop? And, could these two perhaps finally discover where they belong?

Session #24

ハード・ラック・ウーマン

SESSION#24

Scenario : Michiko Yokote
Continuity : Tensai Okamura
Director : Hirokazu Yamada

Women

1 Faye watches the video of her younger self, again, trying to ascertain where it may have been taken. She notes an elevated highway, an airplane; and when she notices a merlion statue, Faye stops the video and stares closely at the screen.

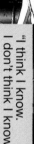

"I think I know. I don't think I know."

2 Ed pops up next to Faye, who is transfixed on the screen. "Water splash," screams Ed. "Eh? You know this place?" Faye asks desperately. "I think I know. I don't think I know. I don't think I know that I know. I think I know even though I don't think I know."

Faye heads for the town in the video!

Faye watches the video that had been sent by her younger self. She doesn't recognize anything in the video, but Ed, who happens to be prying, says that she recognizes the place.

In hyperspace heading for Mars, the Bebop re-routes to Earth and Ed leads Faye to some sort of settlement. But it isn't the place she's looking for, it's a place Ed had lived two years prior. There, Ed and Faye learn about Ed's father before embarking again on a search for the location in the video. When they finally find it, Sally, a former classmate of Faye's, now an old woman, calls out to Faye. She seemed to know about Faye's past, but Faye can only recognize little fragments. Faye says goodbye to Sally, and then returns to the Bebop with Ed.

SESSION#24

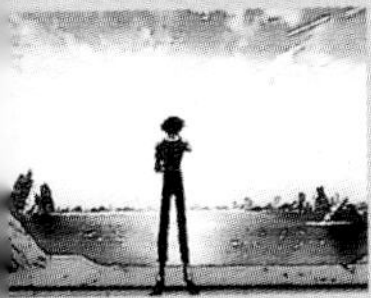

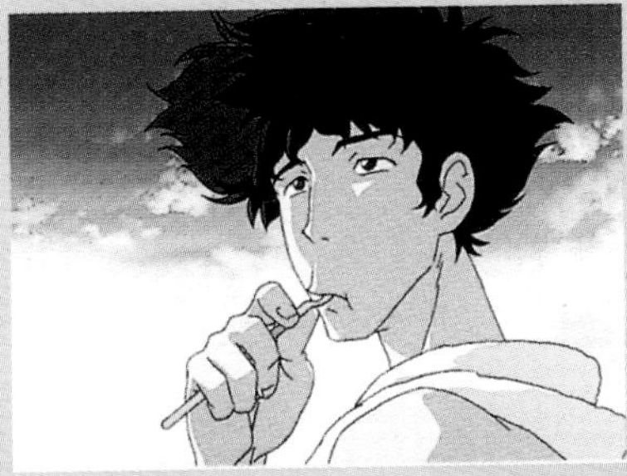

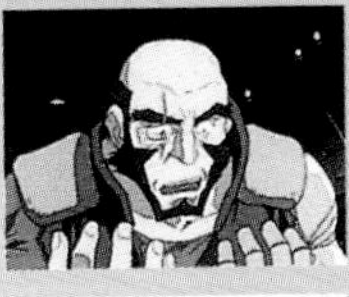

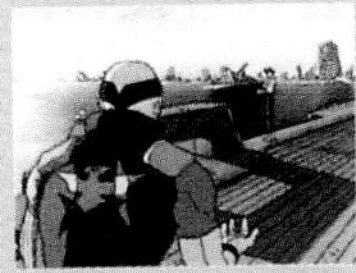

3 "Hey, Spike! Where is this place?" "Earth, isn't it?" "Earth? This ship was supposed to be headed for Mars! How did we end up on Earth all of a sudden?" "Dunno." Finally Spike states calmly, "Jet." "Yeah?" "The women are gone." "Wha?"

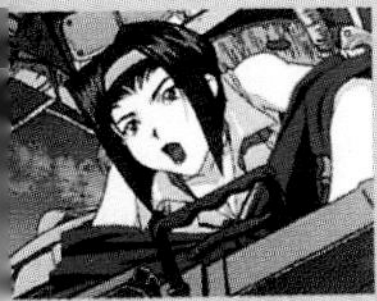

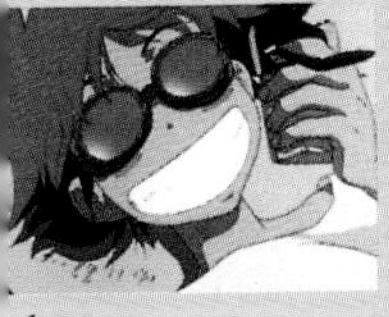

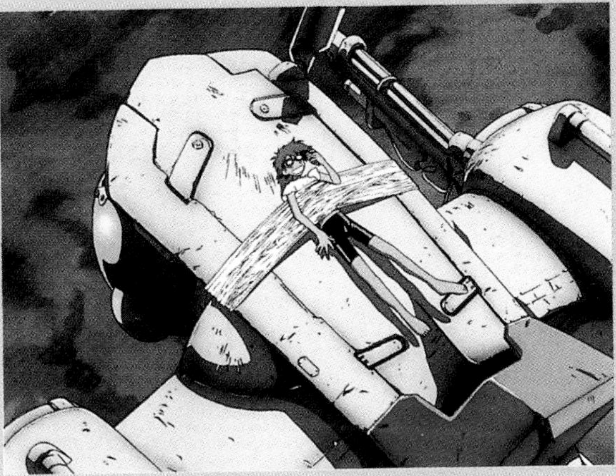

4 "Listen, Ed, if you lead me to the water splash place, I'll give you something good." Tantalized by Faye's words, Ed is tied to the Redtail and leads Faye to the place in the video.

"Something very amazingly tremendously good."

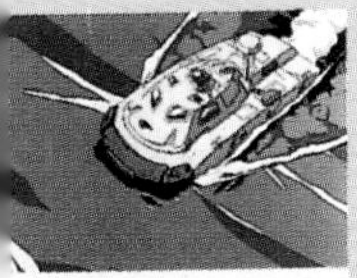

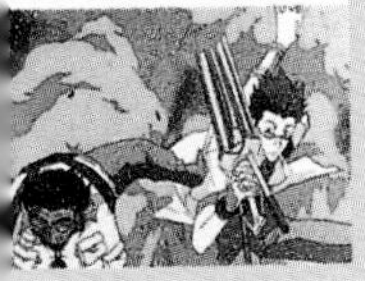

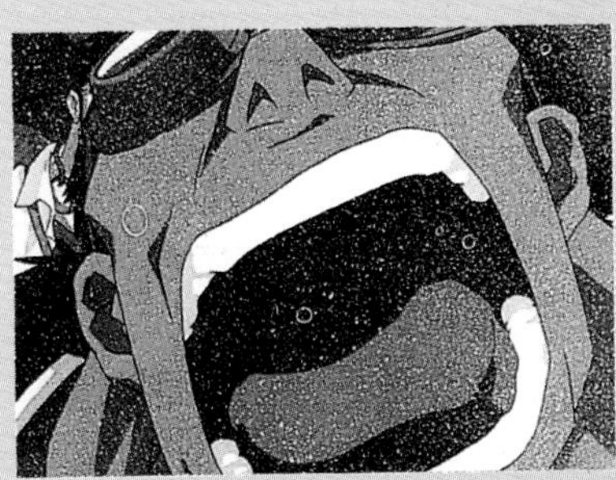

5 Appledelhi and his assistant, MacIntire, two amateur geologists ride across the terrain. Equipped with pickaxes and measuring equipment, these two explore fresh impact craters. They find one to enter, but are immediately repelled by the heat.

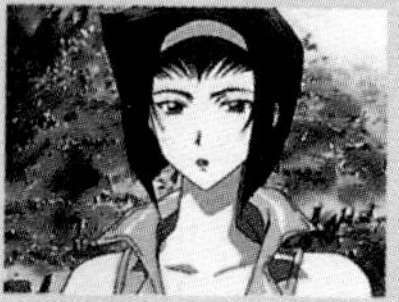

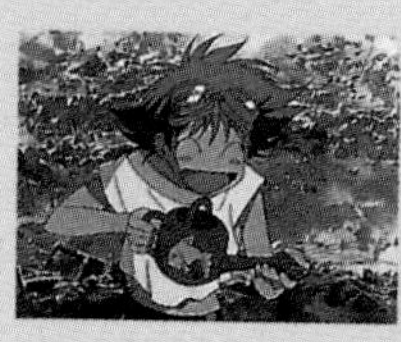

6 A settlement underneath garbage dump. Ed finds a watering can amidst the junk. "Look! Water splash!" Faye hangs here head and grumbles, "......I knew I shouldn't have counted on you."

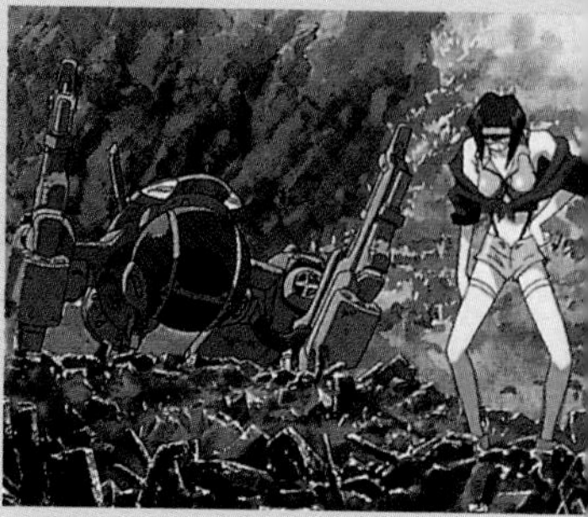

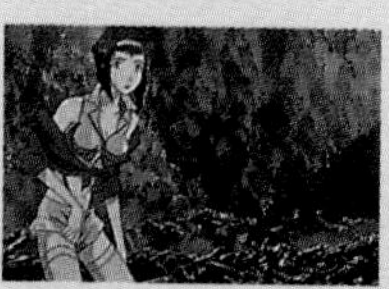

7 As Faye heads back to the Redtail, children poke their heads out all around her. One of them points at Ed and yells, "Ah, I found Ed!" "Huh? Ed has been found?" "What? You know her?"

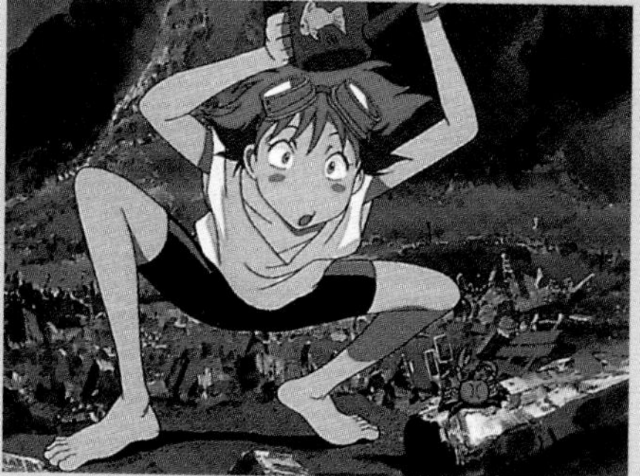

"Ah, I found Ed!"
"Ed's been found?!"

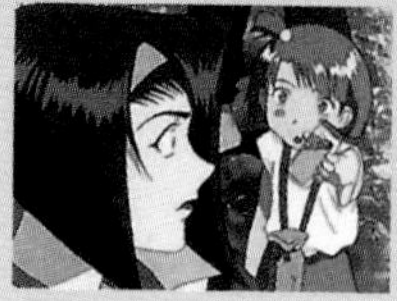

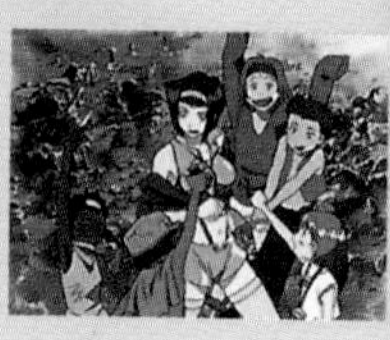

8 Faye seems a little creeped out by being surrounded by children. One of them calls out, "Can I have a fingernail, please!" "Fingernail?" "I collect them. Please! Even just the little finger? C'mon! Please! Please!" "What ARE you kids?" Just then a sharp voice yells at them.

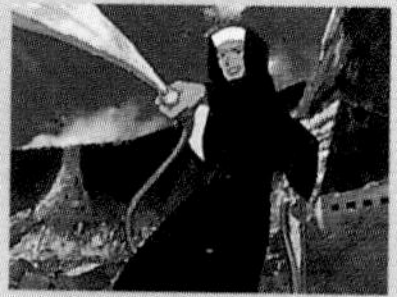

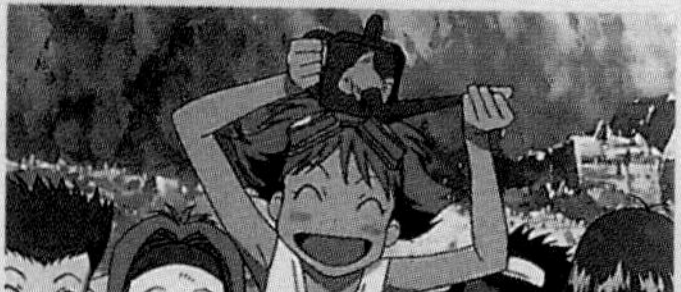

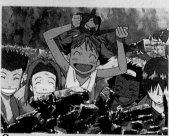

9 The voice's owner, Sister Clara, sprays water at the kids, but ends up hitting Faye dead-on. Clara notices Ed amongst the children and is surprised. "Hmm...? Ah....?! Ed......?!" "Eh heh heh." "It couldn't be...Ed?"

Appledelhi

His full name is Appledelhi Sinis Hesap Lutfen. He makes maps of the earth to (in his own words) "bring back a peaceful peace and non-chaos." He has a dynamic personality, doesn't worry about details, and is strong as an ox. He supports himself and seems to squeeze out a meager living from occassionally selling his map data to the Earth government.

SESSION#24

10 Faye and Clara talk. "Five years ago, Ed just wandered in, and before I knew it, had made herself at home. About three years ago she just wandered off." Faye listens intently to the story.

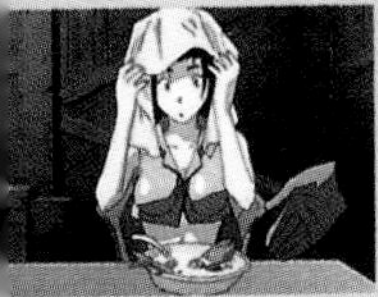
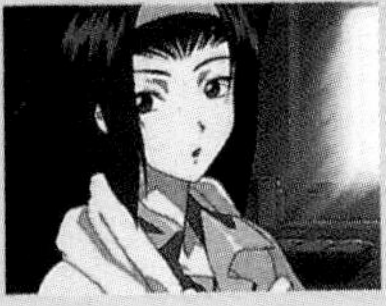
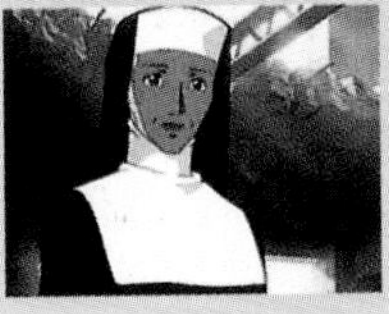

"We just came here to get some food."
"……Look, you."

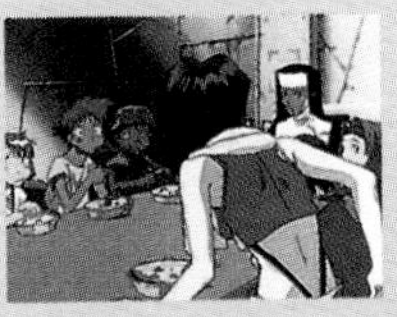
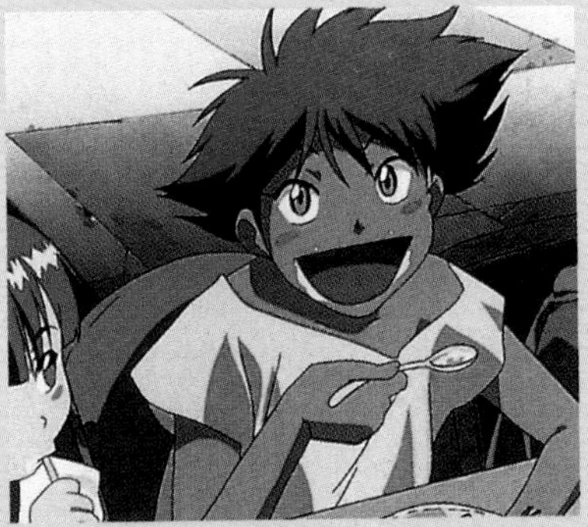

11 Dinner is served, but Faye stands to go. "I…I need to be going." "What? Already?" "I'm looking for something…" "Ed knows where it is!" When Ed says that, Faye loses her strength. "We just came here to get some food." "……Look, you." "You're gonna give me something really good, right?"

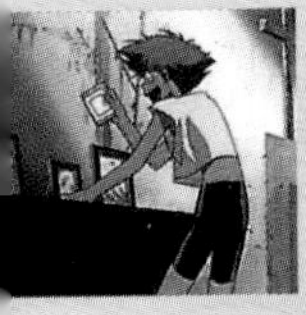
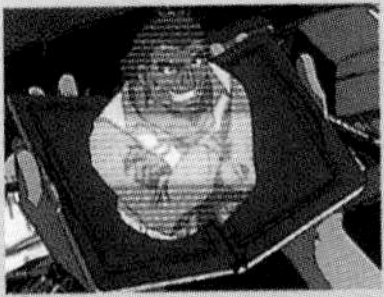
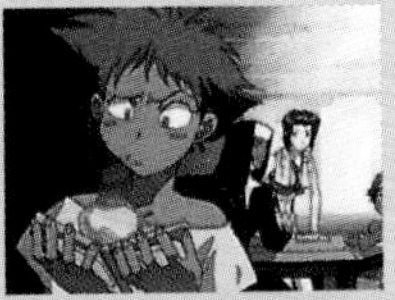

12 Clara remembers something. "Oh yeah, Ed. That desk. There's something good in the drawer." "Something good?" Ed takes out a hologram of Appledelhi. "It's her father." "Wh, who?" "It was no more than two months ago that he came here looking for Ed. He forgot that he had left her at the day care center." Ed stared at the hologram.

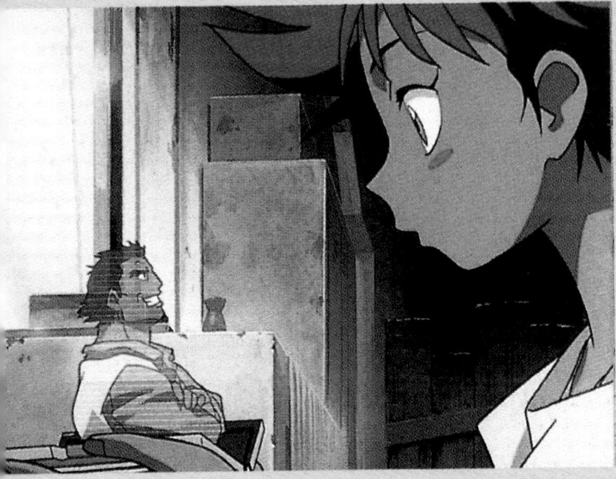

"I hope she will be able to see him…"

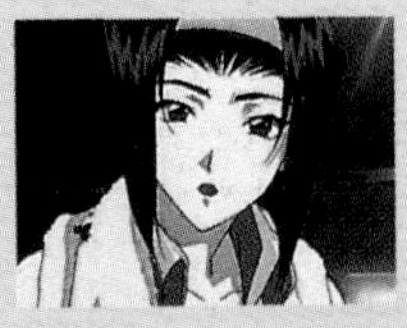

13 Appledelhi digs a hole at the bottom of a crater with a pickaxe. MacIntire puts some sort of device into the hole which updates the map information. MacIntire smiles at the result and Appledelhi grins widely.

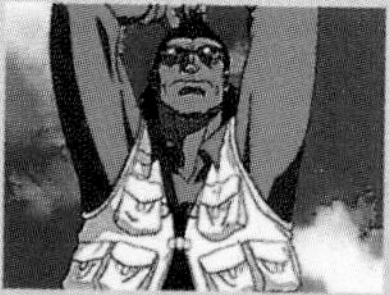

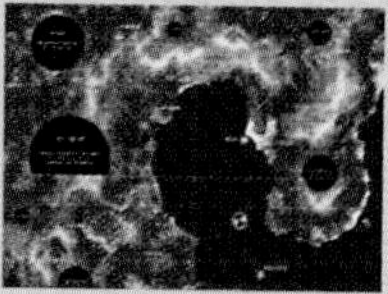

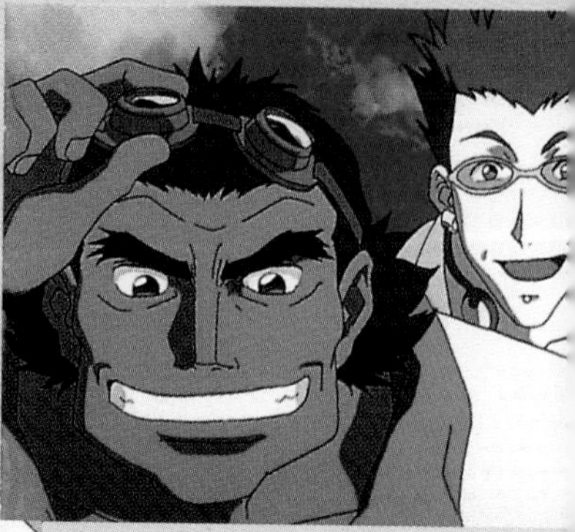

"You're......Faye?"

14 When Faye reaches the place in the video, an old woman calls out to her. "Are you... Faye? No... Is it really you?" "Ah..." "It's me, Sally Young! I was your classmate in high school!"

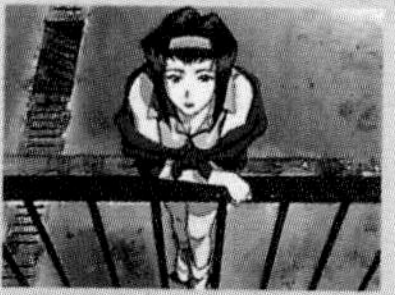

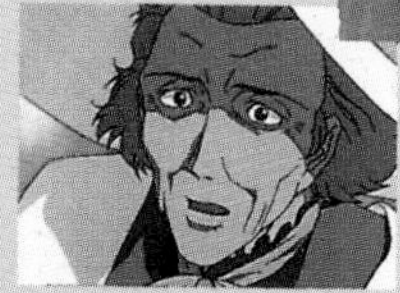

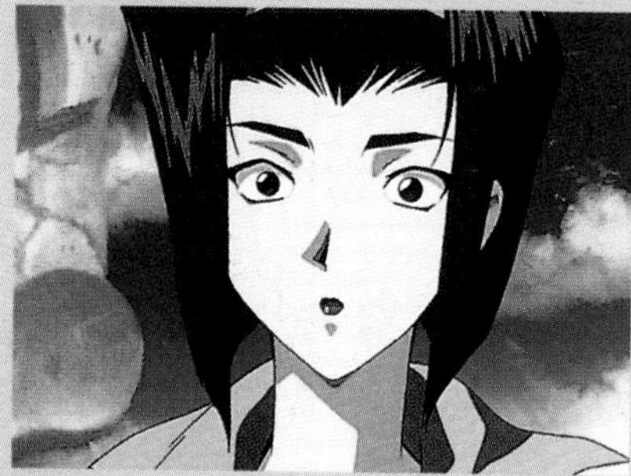

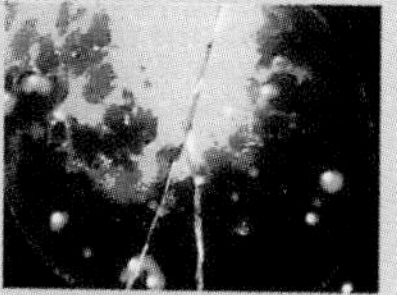

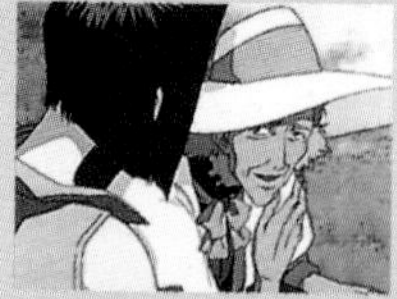

"Accident?"
"Faye, you don't remember?"
"I...I..."

INTERLUDE

Appledelhi, one of the strongest characters in "Bebop." "He doesn't have much to do with good or evil. He's not just an easy-going guy, he's a big guy on a grand scale who thinks about things on a universal scale," says Bebop's director, Shinchiro Watanabe. When Appledelhi sees Ed, he yells out "Francoise!" but seeing as he's the kind of person who forgets the sex of his own child, it's doubtful this is Ed's real name.

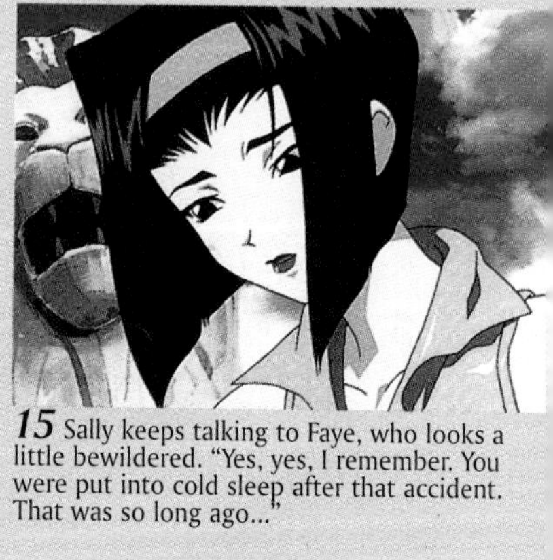

15 Sally keeps talking to Faye, who looks a little bewildered. "Yes, yes, I remember. You were put into cold sleep after that accident. That was so long ago..."

SESSION#24

16 "Do you know who
his is? Probably not,
ight? Well, she's......"
ally starts to introduce
aye to the young girl
vho comes to see her.
But Faye smiles and
ays, "a ghost."

"Do you know who this is?"
"Ummm..."
"Probably not, right? Well, she's..." "A ghost."

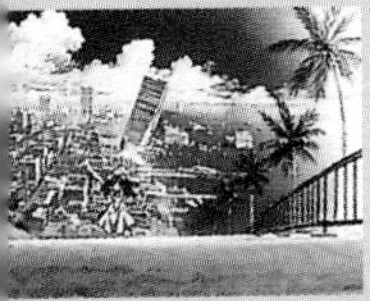

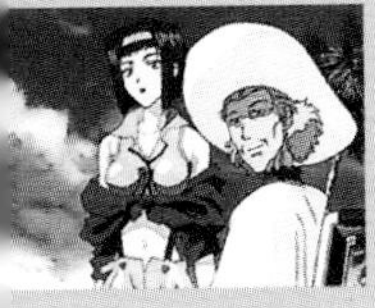

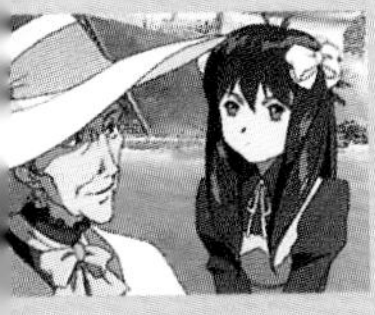

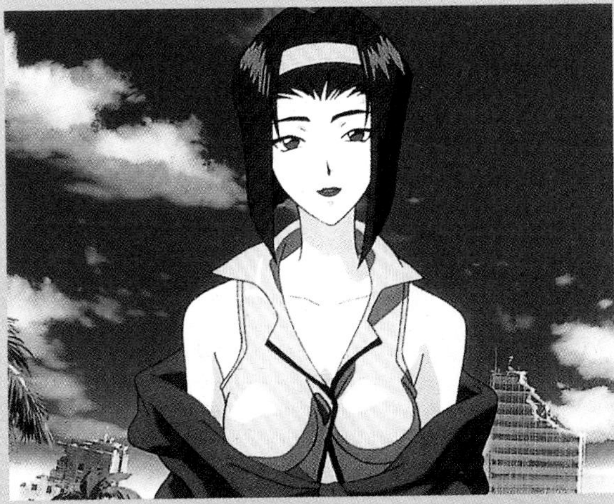

17 Faye smiles and tells Sally, "Goodbye. Take care." She grabs Ed, who seems stuck in a squat, and runs off. Sally and the little girl stare at Faye and Ed as the two rush away.

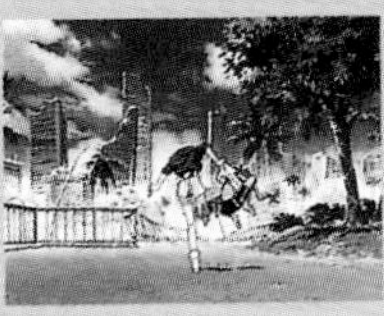

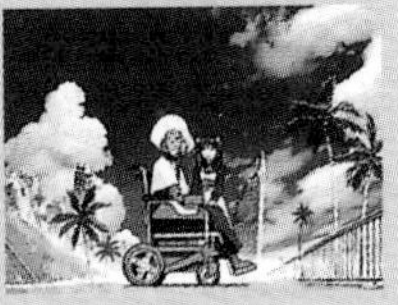

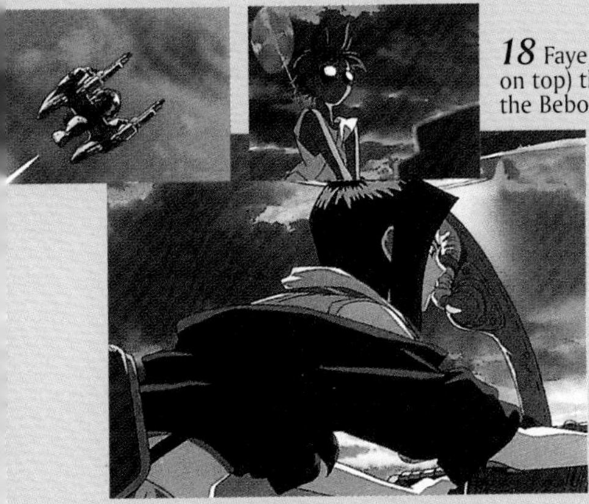

18 Faye pilots the Redtail (with Ed sitting on top) through the twilight sky back to the Bebop, a dazed look on her face.

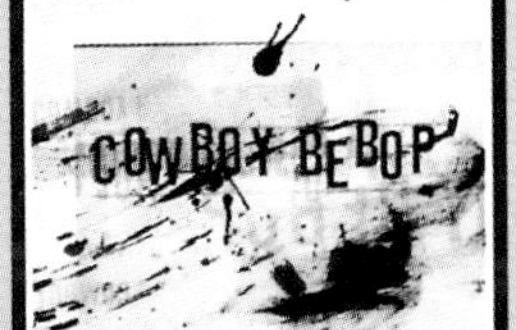
COWBOY BEBOP

EYE CATCH

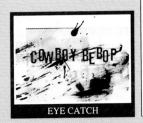

19 Jet yells at Faye when she returns. "Ah, so it's you guys! Why'd you change course? Our plans are completely ruined because of it! I don't appreciate your doing things like that without asking first." But they notice Faye doesn't seem her usual self, a pensive pall muscling out her usual wry humor.

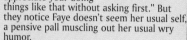

"Wanna see something real good?"

20 Ein walks up to Ed, who is fiddling around on the computer. "Hmm…? Wanna see something reeeal good?" Ed shows him the hologram of Appledelhi. Meanwhile, Faye is back in her room, collapsed on the bed, her face awash with sorrow and pain.

Faye's memories return! Ed is reunited with her father!

Faye and Ed return to the Bebop. With a brooding expression on her face, Faye goes to her room and flops down on the bed. Jet and Spike can't hide their confusion over Faye's odd behavior. Faye gets out of bed and into the shower. Suddenly, though her body doesn't move an inch, her eyes fly wide open. She's remembered something: memories that she couldn't recall before, about her school days and a shuttle accident. Consumed with emotion, Faye returns to the Redtail to go back to "where I belong."

21 "Maybe they're just too hungry. People act a bit strange when they haven't had food to eat." Jet is worried about Faye and Ed's behavior. Spike doesn't worry though, and just checks some information on a bounty. "50 million, huh?" "Hnnn? Whoa, that's big. Appledelhi Sinis Hesap Lutfen, huh?"

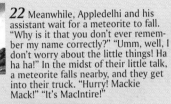

"Do you want a smoke too,
MacEnroe?"
"It's MacIntire.
And no thanks, Mr. Appledelhi."

22 Meanwhile, Appledelhi and his assistant wait for a meteorite to fall. "Why is it that you don't ever remember my name correctly?" "Umm, well, I don't worry about the little things! Ha ha ha!" In the midst of their little talk, a meteorite falls nearby, and they get into their truck. "Hurry! Mackie Mack!" "It's MacIntire!"

23 Faye wakes up and gets into the shower. Just then, memories begin to surface. The merlion statue, school, the stuffed animals in her room, her school backpack, young Sally, a fountain in a garden, herself riding in a shuttle, and then an accident. Her dormant memories have suddenly re-awakened.

24 Faye turns off the water and hurries out of the shower, then runs out of the bathroom, bumping into Spike. "Sorry." "SORRY?" "I… I…I have to go." Faye runs out.

"I… I…
I have to go…"

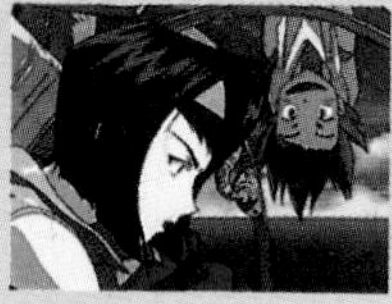

25 When Faye gets into the Redtail, Ed asks her, “Where ya goin'?” “I remembered where I belong.” “Where you belong?” “Someone is waiting for you, too… you have a place where you belong too, so you should go look for it.”

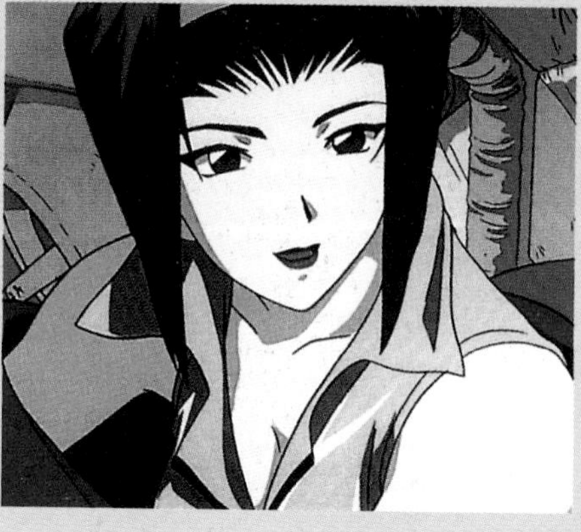

“Where ya goin'?”
“I remembered where I belong.”

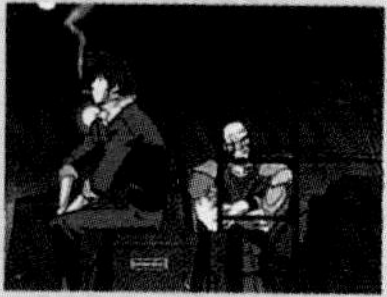

26 “If you're talking about Faye, she left.” “Again?” Spike asks, “Hey, where did she go this time…” but Jet doesn't know. “……Women are as fickle as the weather on Ganymede, eh?”

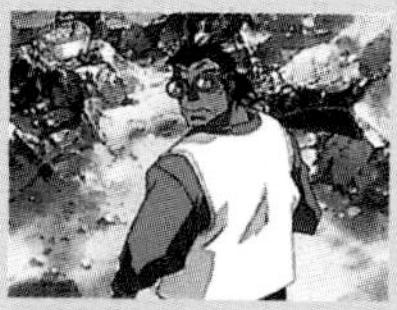

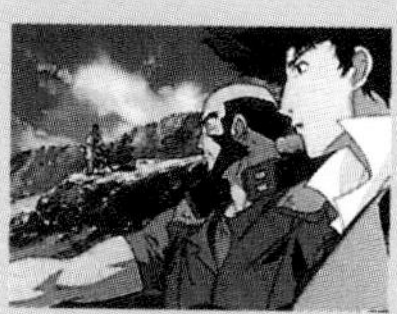

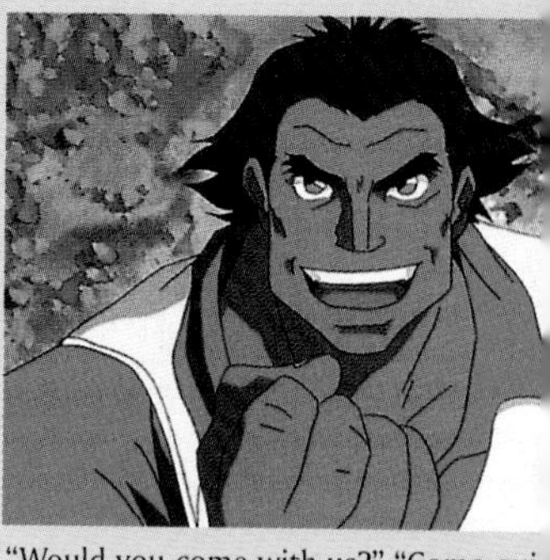

27 “Appledelhi, right?” “Would you come with us?” “Come quietly if you don't want to get hurt.” Spike and Jet aim their guns at Appledelhi. But he doesn't move. “On this Earth ruled by chaos, what do you think we need to restore a peaceful peace and non-chaos?” “Huh?” “MAPS, maps!”

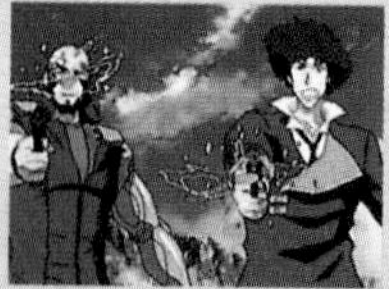

28 Before Spike can answer, Appledelhi launches a strike. In a fit of rage, Spike pounces on Appledelhi, but his attack has absolutely no effect.

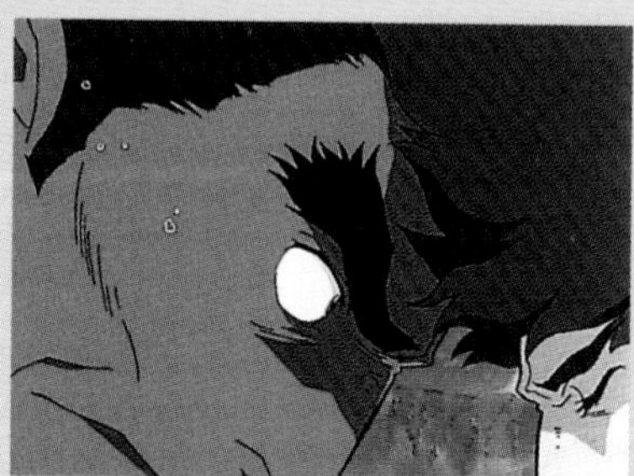

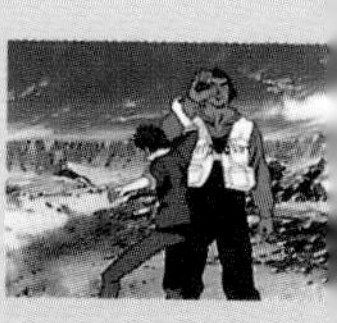

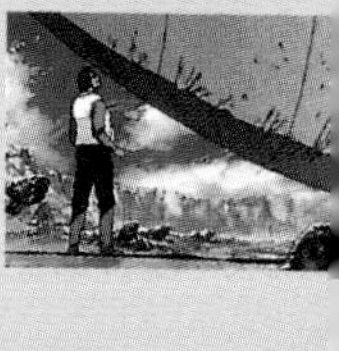

SESSION#24

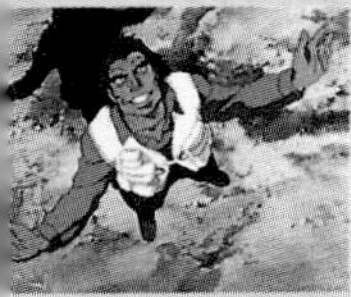

"Francoise!"

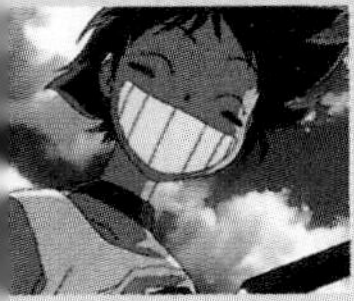

9 Ed interrupts the ust just as Spike and ppledelhi are fight- ıg. When Appledelhi ees Ed, he opens his rms up to her. ppledelhi is Ed's ther! Ed gets a ough-housing recep- on from her dad.

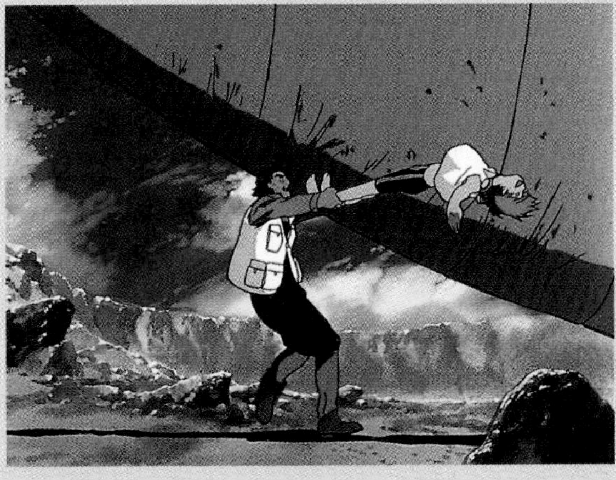

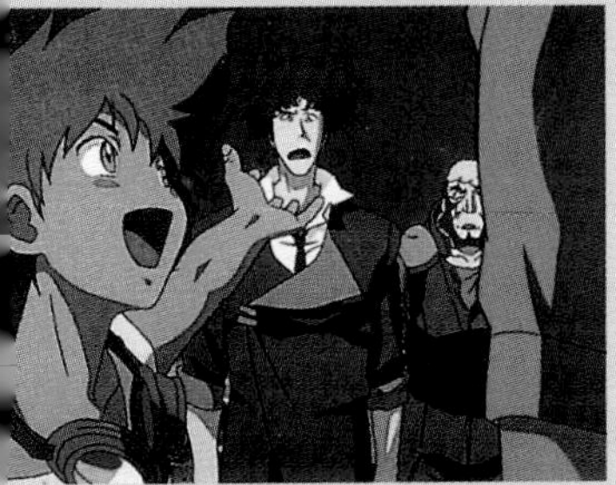

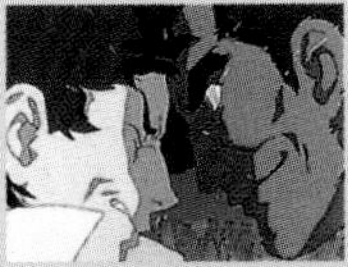

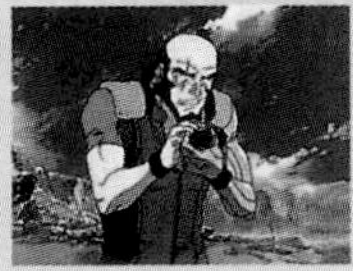

30 Ed begins to introduce everyone. "This is my father-person," she explains. "That's Spike-person and that's Jet-person." "Is that so?" Appledelhi head-butts Spike, but Ed scolds him, "No, father! He's a nice man." "Hmm? Is that so?" It was Ed who put the bounty on Appledelhi, and it was actually only 50 woolongs.

"Father!"

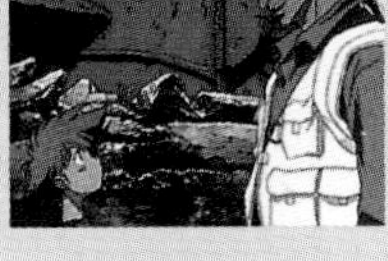

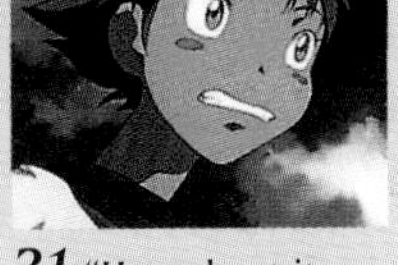

31 "How about it, are you going to come with me?" "What…?" Ed is bewildered by the invitation before Appledelhi sees another meteorite crash and rushes off.

"…He's gone."

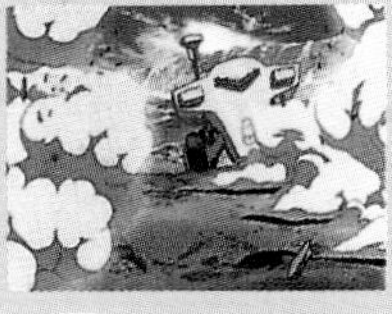

MacIntire

Appledelhi's assistant. Appledelhi never calls him by his correct name, a condition MacIntire has resigned himself to. He has a real passion for making maps. Until he teamed up with Appledelhi, he plodded around jobless. He was deeply impressed by Appledelhi's personality and ideas, and so afterwards, MacIntire followed him around until he was hired as an assistant. It goes without saying, there are a lot of strange people on earth. He's probably about 20-years-old.

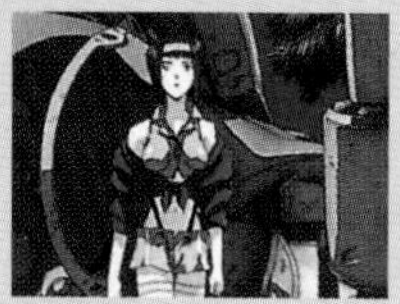
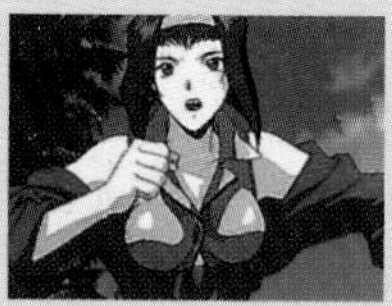
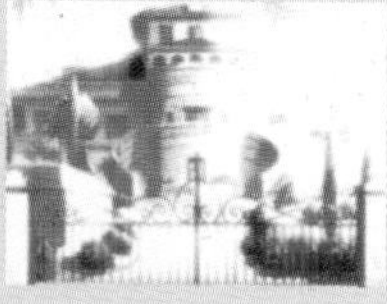

32 Faye visits a place that may very well have been her home. She runs until she's almost out of breath, up the stairs leading to a house straight out of her childhood memories. She reaches the house, but...

33 Faye stands dumbstruck in front of a ruined building. The grounds are dilapidated, and only a trace of the house remains. The merlion statue in the fountain, a landmark of the house, is in ruins as well. Faye can only look around in a daze, unable to move.

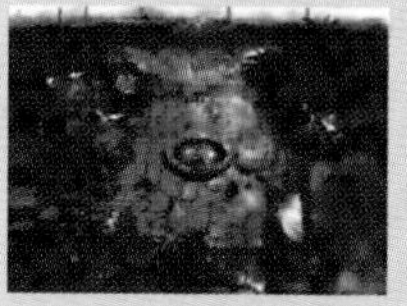
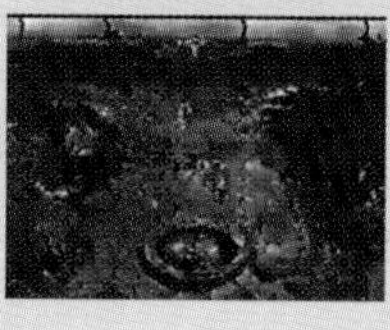
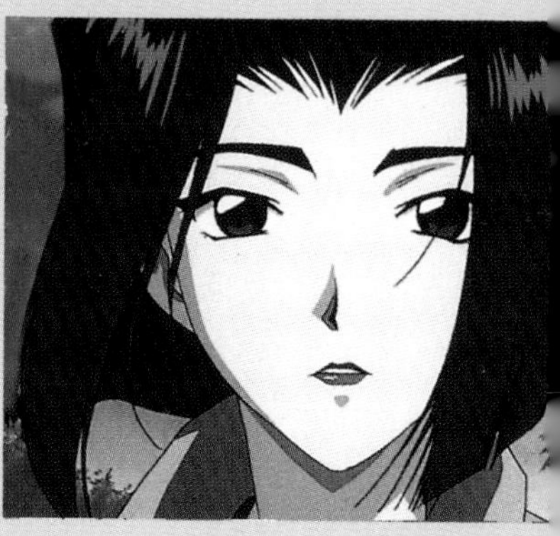

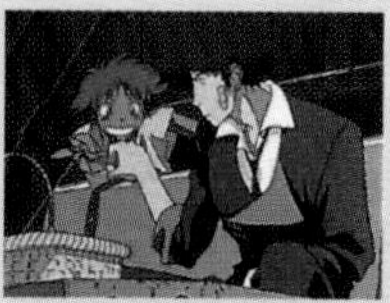
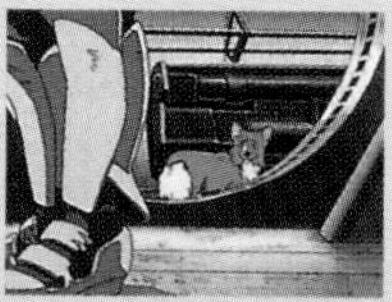

34 Meanwhile, on the Bebop, Ed offers a pinwheel to Spike. He accepts it with a confused expression on his face. Ein passes under Jet's feet as he makes dinner. Ready for dinner, Jet goes to get Spike only to find his partner staring at a message scrawled on the deck.

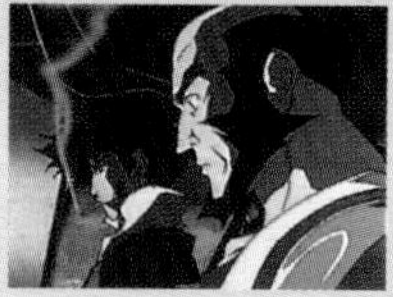
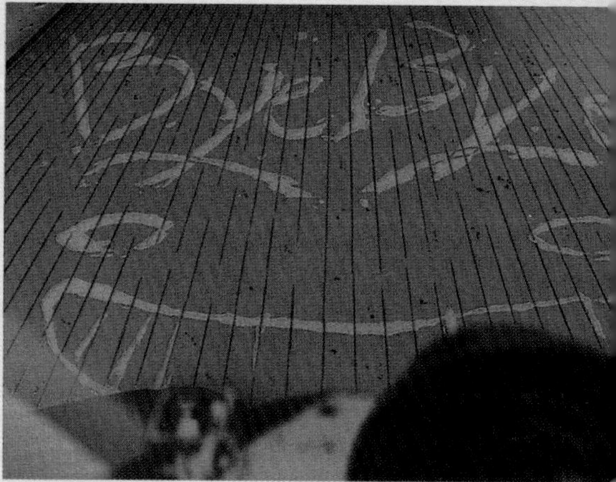

SESSION# 24

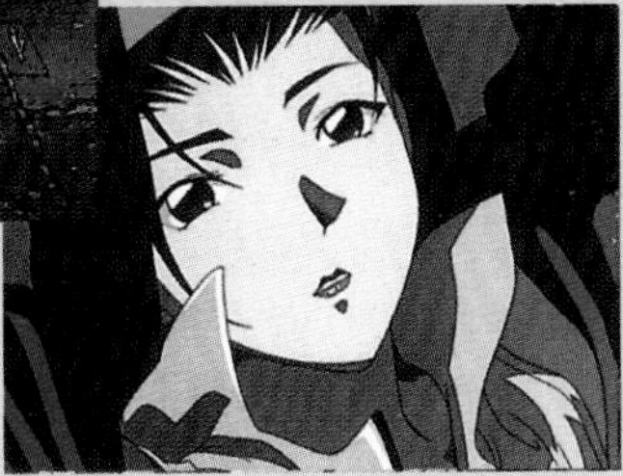

35 Faye draws lines on the ground that mark where rooms in the house once stood. Faye lays down in the remains of her room, inside lines that mark where her bed once met a windowed wall.

INTERLUDE

When Ed leaves the Bebop, she gives a pinwheel to Spike. Ed brought it back with her from the convent. It's a tradition for the children of the convent to leave pinwheels to mark the places they visit.

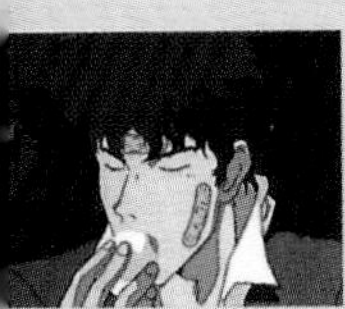

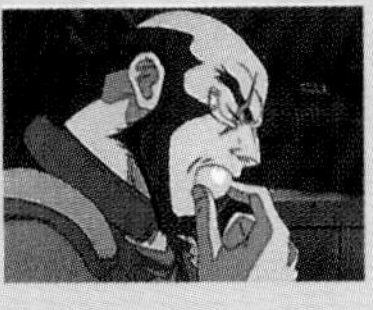

36 Appledelhi had given Spike and Jet eggs s a token of thanks for looking after Ed. hey are all now boiled for dinner, divided mongst four plates lying on the living room able. Spike and Jet stuff their faces.

"Ed is going far, far away. I might not be coming back again."

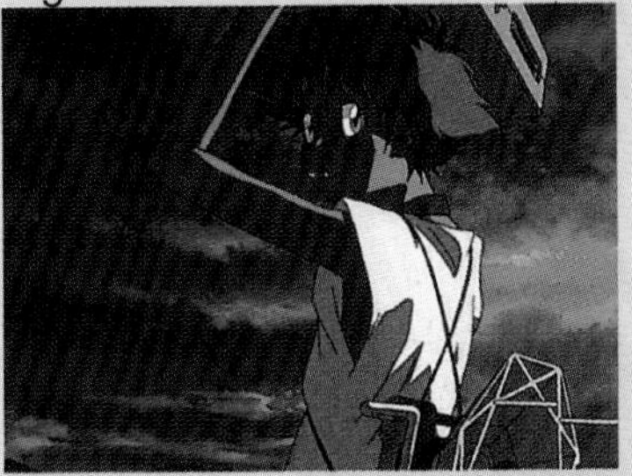

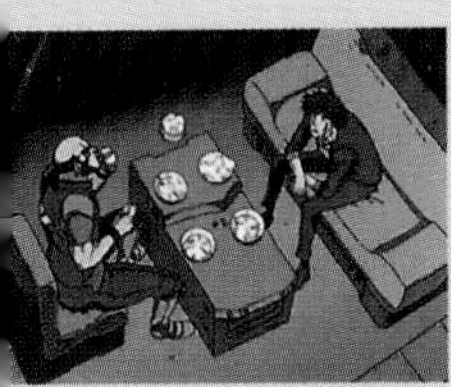

38 Spike and Jet continue ating. Having eaten their wn share, they start on the ther plages... and the meal ontinues without a word…

37 Ein follows Ed as she leaves the Bebop behind. "You can't come with me, Ein." "Whine…" "Ed is going far away. I probably won't come back again." Ein looks sad, so Ed asks, "…Do you wanna come with Ed?"

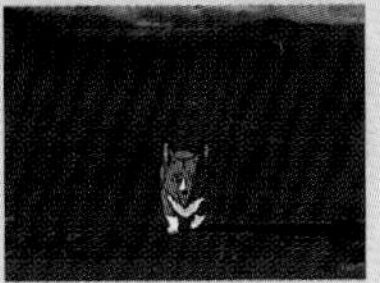

39 Ed stops and looks back at the Bebop. But then, she calls out "Let's go, Ein!" and starts running across the wasteland. The pinwheel Ed gave to Spike sits atop the Bebop's bow, as if bidding them farewell.

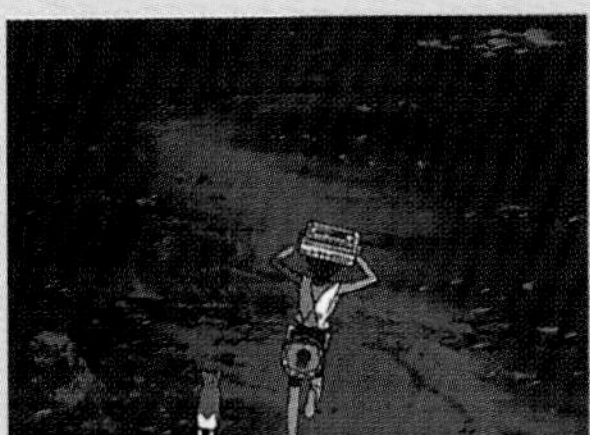

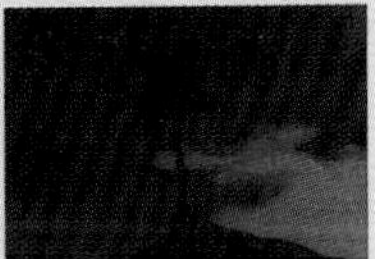

SEE YOU COWGIRL, SOMEDAY, SOMEWHERE

The Real Fo

Vicious finally begins his coup, positioning himself to assume leadership of the Red Dragon Syndicate. Gunshots ring like the sound of a choir of angels, a premonition of damnation. Knowing that the Red Dragon's civil war has begun, Julia breaks her long silence and tries to contact Spike, who drops everything to find her, the only woman who could complete this hollow man. At the fulcrum of a fragile balance, Spike is possessed by the spirits of his past. Jet and Faye can do nothing but watch over him. Jerked awake from his nightmare, Spike needs to once again confront Vicious, and Julia, for no other reason than to convince himself that they are not merely just remnants of a bad dream.

Session#25

ザ・リアル・フォークブルース
（前編）

SESSION#25

Scenario : Keiko Nobumoto
Continuity: Shinichirou Watanabe
Director : Ikurou Satou

lues (Part 1)

1 Mars. On a street in the rain, a woman with a red umbrella. It is Julia. She makes her way to her apartment. She gets a message on the phone. "The elders are going to move. You are in danger as well. Please, hurry."

2 Vicious and his men attack the Red Dragon headquarters. Unhappy with being judged unfit as the successor to the syndicate, Vicious has begun a rebellion against the elders. But the rebellion fails. All of his plans have been leaked.

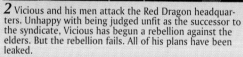

The wheels of fate begin to move with Vicious' revolt.

Unhappy with the way the Red Dragons have begun sliding to the moderate, Vicious rebe against the elders in order to seize real power within the syndicate. But his plans were leake to the elders, and his coup fails. He's taken into custody…

Meanwhile, Red Dragon assassins attack Spike and Jet while they try to enjoy a drink at a ba But Shin, the younger brother of Lin, who was once Vicious' subordinate and a friend to Spik come to the rescue. In the midst of their escape, Shin tells Spike about Vicious, and abo Julia's life being in danger. They duck out of sight and visit a Doctor to attend to Jet's wound Jet, who can't move, warns Spike not to get involved with the syndicate anymore, but…

Around this time, Faye returns to Mars and receives a message from Spike asking her to con back to pick them up. She cuts it off before it even finishes. But almost immediately after tha a blonde woman in dark glasses and a convertible approaches Faye!

The elders thwart cious' coup tempt. "The for- ne teller told us at on the night of e red moon, the ake will strike." o Long continues, ou look so pitiful, cious."

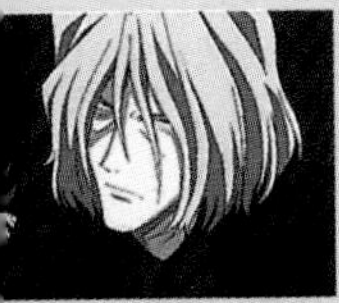

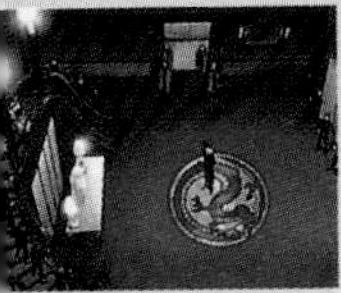

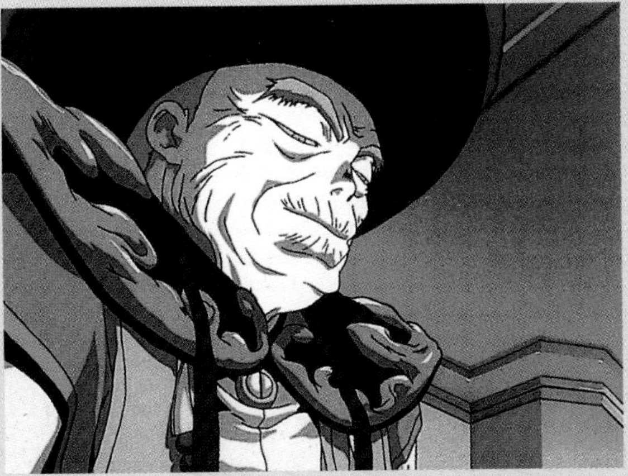

"What a foolish act you have committed."

Pin Long says, "We have told you of our decision that ou cannot be our successor." Vicious answers, "The yndicate has no use for corpses that can't even fight." ooking down on Vicious from above, Wang Long tells m, "Your arrogance will be your undoing."

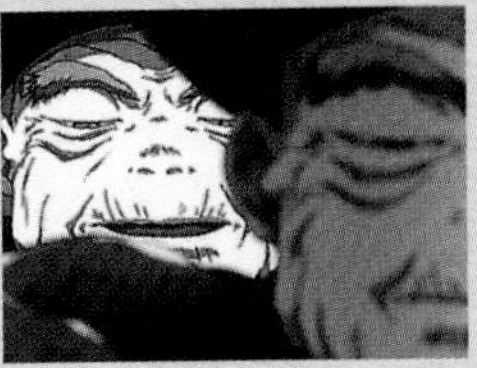

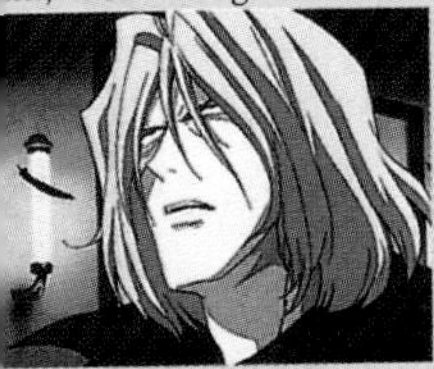

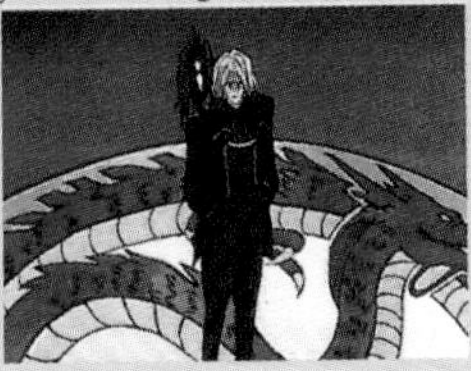

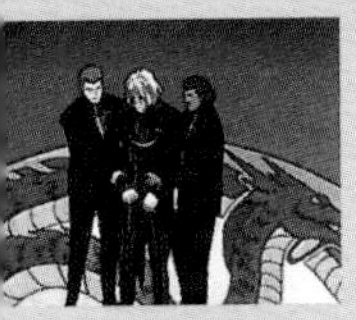

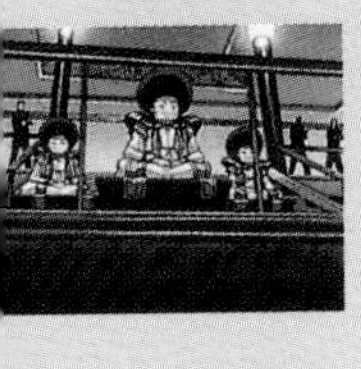

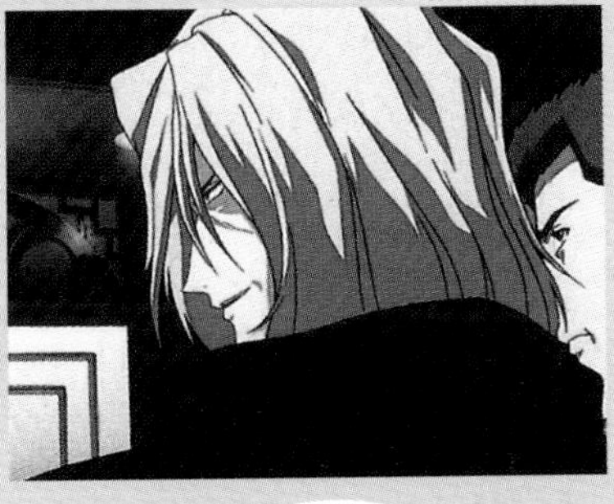

5 Wang Long orders Vicious be taken to the judgment room. Vicious glares at Wang Long and says, "Kill me. Now." Wang Long grins. "You cannot choose your death. Only after we have let you taste humiliation, will we send you to the underworld." As he is taken away, Vicious tells the elders, "Don't forget. A snake's poison can work slowly."

6 Spike and Jet drink at a dingy bar. Jet complains that the hole left by Faye and Ed has caused them to bungle their jobs. Spike listens to his grumbling but doesn't really pay much attention. Suddenly he senses an uneasy atmosphere outside, and lifts his head…

"There's too much Vermouth."

7 Jet notices it too. The two dive behind the bar just as a hail of bullets penetrate the air. The two bounty hunters return fire. Spike takes a moment to complain about the cocktail the bartender made, but the enemy keeps showering them with bullets!

8 In the middle of the fierce gun battle, Jet demands of Spike to know who these guys are then takes a bullet in the thigh!

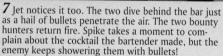

INTERLUDE

Shin, the younger brother of Lin, who appeared in Session 12~13, makes his appearance in this session. These two brothers were both Spike's subordinates when he was in the Red Dragons. But when Spike disappeared, they both fell under Vicious' authority. When Lin died in Session 13 though, Shin felt that it was Vicious' fault, and afterwards put distance between himself and the Red Dragons: both Vicious and the elders.

SESSION#25

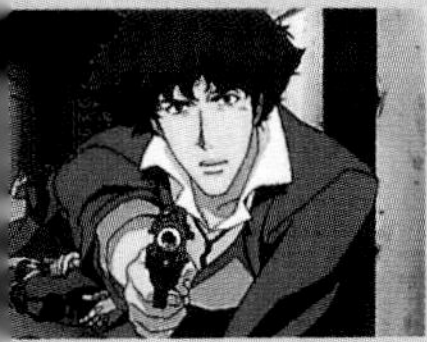
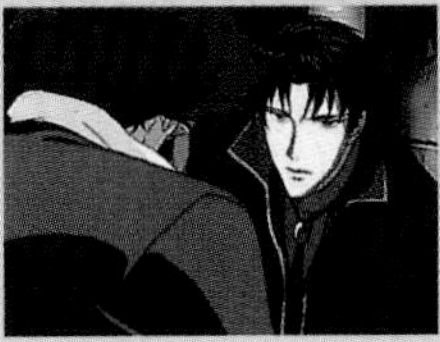

9 Just as Spike goes to return fire, the enemy falls lead. Standing behind him is a familiar face: Shin, he younger brother of Lin, who was Vicious' right and man. He covers Spike and Jet's escape. Spike ells Lin, "If you side with me you won't be able to eturn to the syndicate."

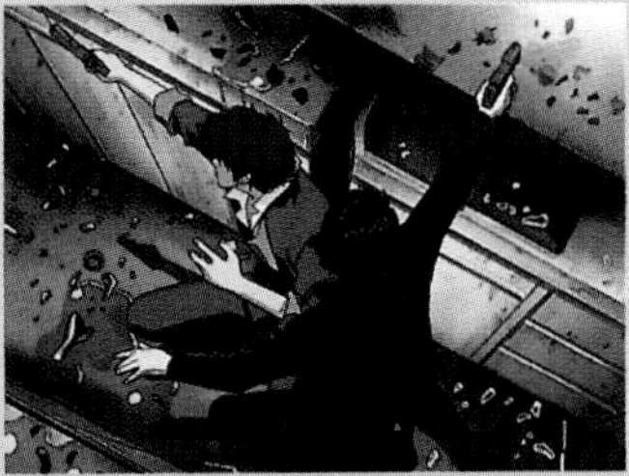
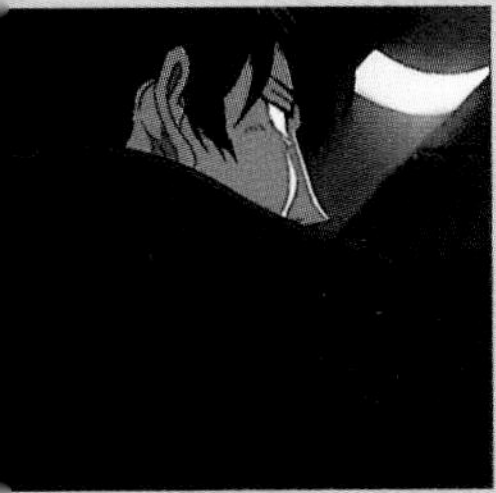
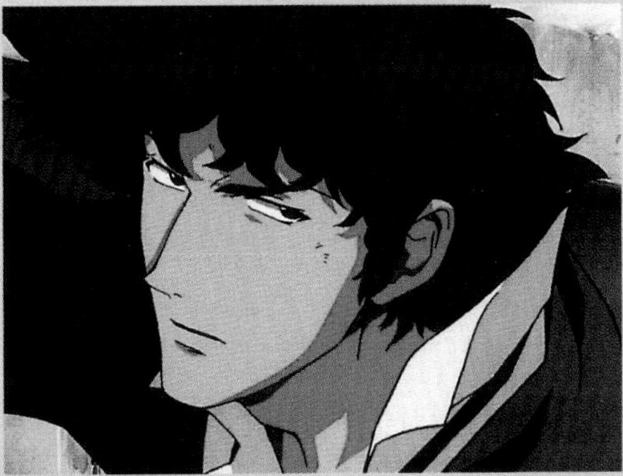

"You're in danger too. And so is Julia."

10 Spike asks Shin "What happened?" Between shots at the enemy, Shin tells Spike that Vicious had attempted a coup d'etat but failed, and had been captured by the elders. "You're in danger too. And so is Julia." Spike is stunned when Shin mentions that name. "Julia?"

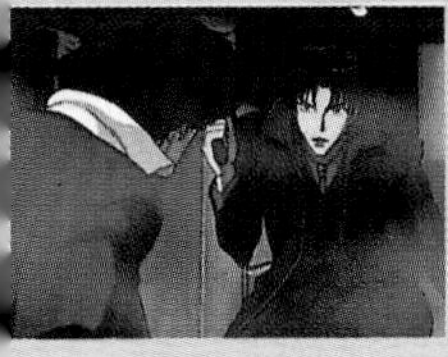
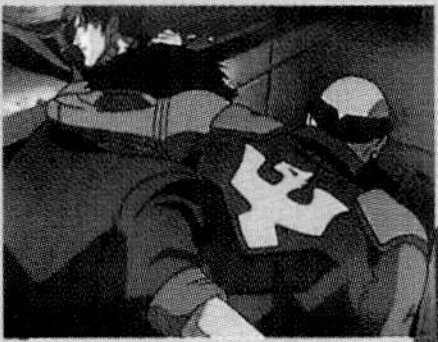
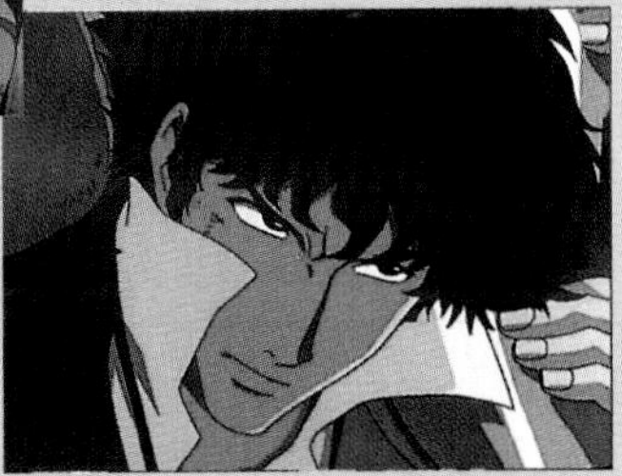

11 Shin tells Spike where Julia is. "She's in the city of Tharsis. I'll hold these guys off here." He urges Spike to, "Please, go." Spike says, "I owe you one, Shin!" Supporting Jet, who can barely walk on his wounded leg, Spike uses the blast from a hand grenade as cover to escape.

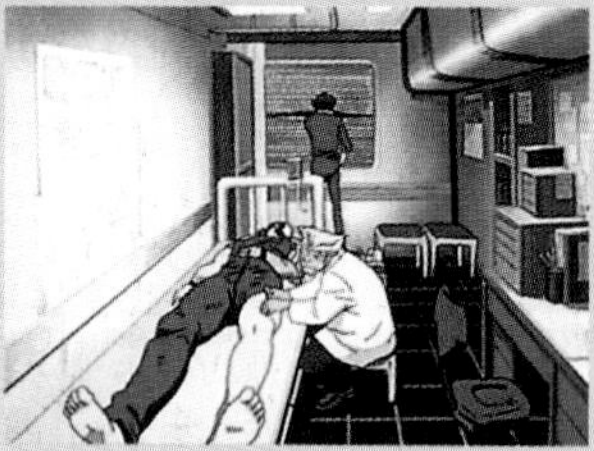
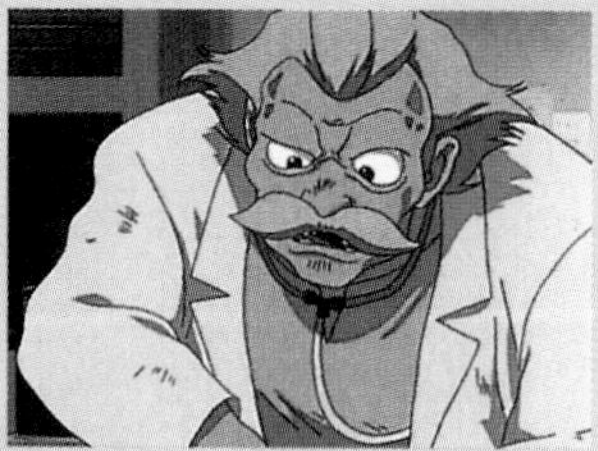

12 Spike and Jet visit the doctor for treatment. Jet, lying on the bed, warns Spike not to get involved with the syndicate anymore. "Vicious. Julia. To me those names are nothing but bad news. Like the words to a magic spell that opens a door that shouldn't be opened."

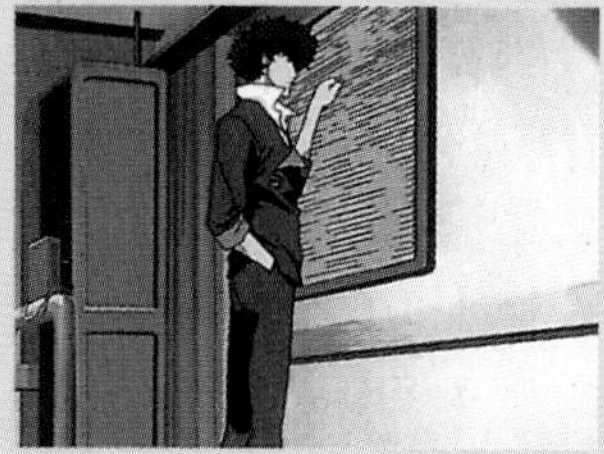
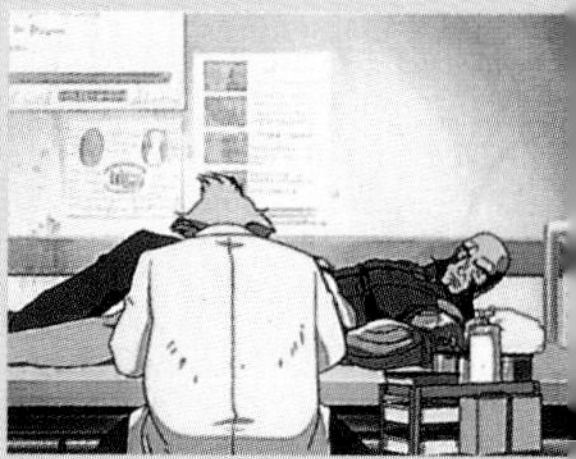

13 Spike tells Jet, "I understand." Jet tells the doctor, "Forget that we came here," and the doctor replies, "I'm just treating some stray cats that came wandering in." Spike remembers the distant past…

"We'll just live a life of freedom somewhere. Just like a dream…"

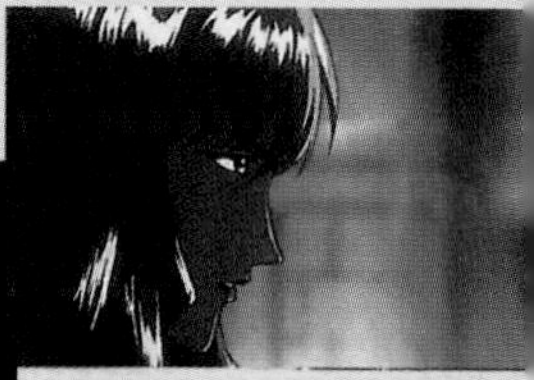
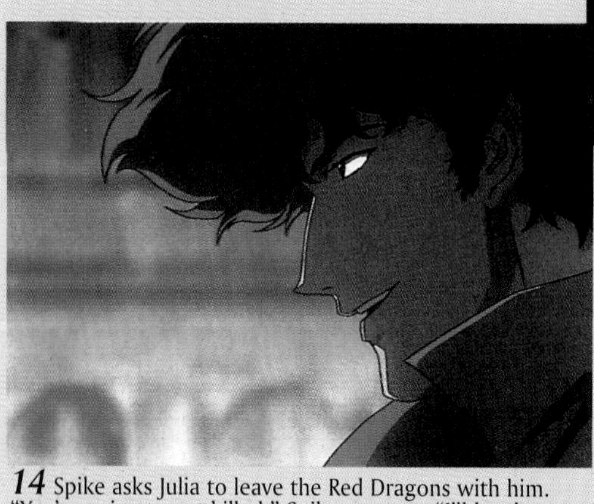
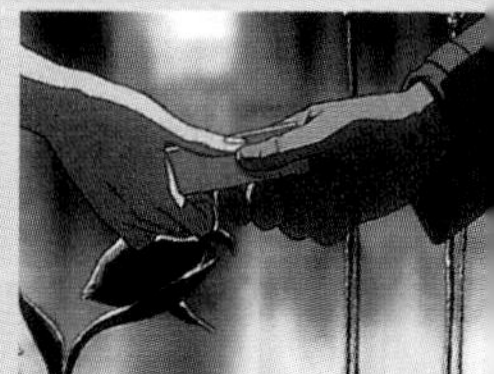
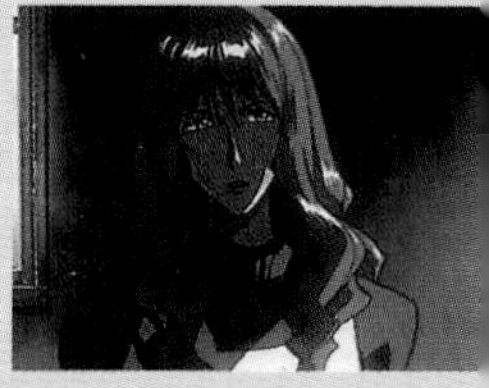

14 Spike asks Julia to leave the Red Dragons with him. "You're going to get killed." Spike answers, "I'll let them think I'm dead." Julia hesitates, "I…can't come with you." Spike holds out a ticket, and says, "We'll escape from this world." Julia asks, "And then what will we do?"

SESSION#25

15 As Spike reminisces, Julia heads somewhere in a red convertible. She relives an incident from the past in her mind: Vicious points a gun at her and asks, "Are you going to betray me? Try to leave this world?"

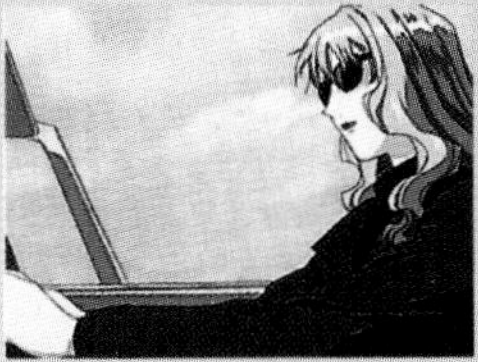

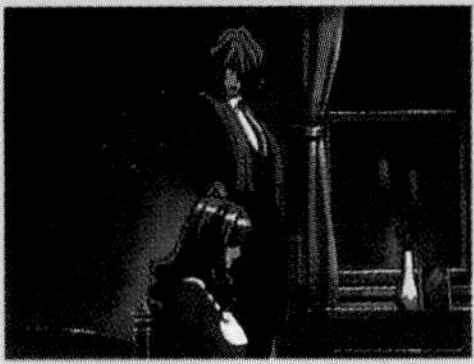

"It's impossible, even in a dream."

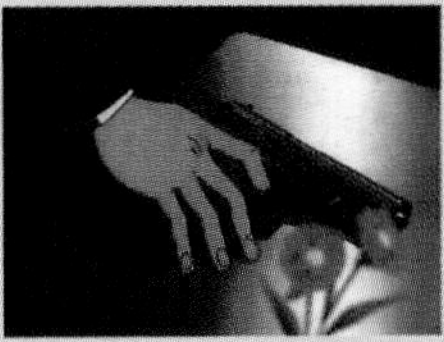

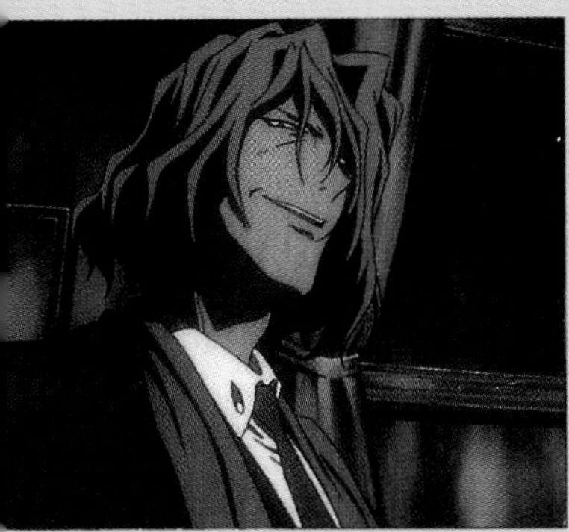

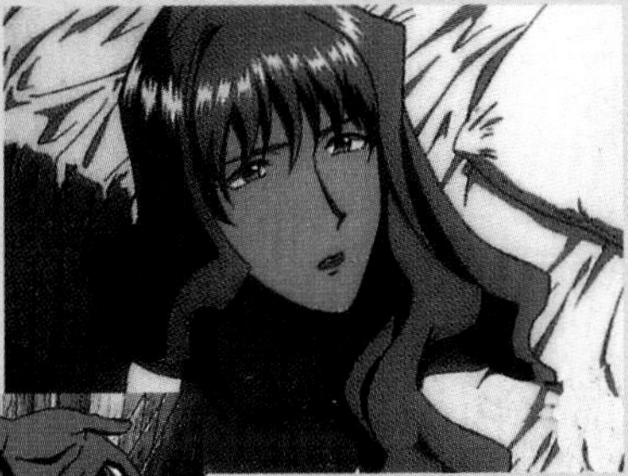

16 Vicious says, "It's impossible to leave." "Is he going to be killed?" Julia asks. Lowering his gun and placing it on the table, Vicious answers, "Yes. By your hand." Shocked, Julia turns to look at him. Vicious tells her coldly, "You stay alive. Or you both die. You will decide." Julia tears up and throws away the ticket.

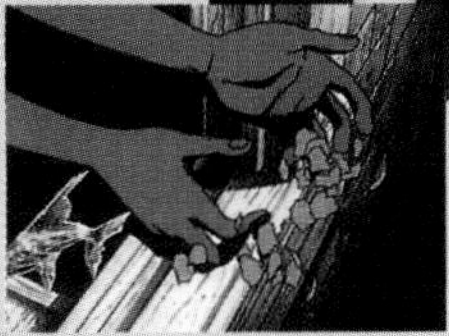

INTERLUDE

Julia was once Vicious' lover, but Spike and Julia ended up falling in love. Spike planned to leave the Red Dragons with Julia, but his plans were discovered by Vicious, who ordered Julia to kill Spike. She disobeys his orders and had to live on the run from the Red Dragons.

17 Captured, Vicious is chained up in the judgment room. He appears to be asleep. But when his eyes slowly open, a belligerent spirit still burns within them, even in such a wretched situation...

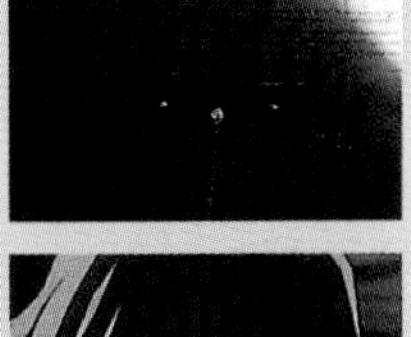

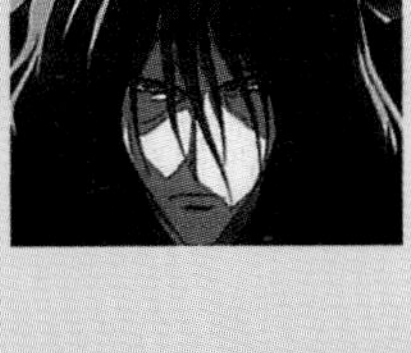

18 Faye stands alone at an airport on Mars, having left the Bebop and trying to decide her next move. When she looks around the lobby, she sees an old woman talking to herself sullenly.

19 "There is no place for me after all," the old woman mumbles. Just then, a man who appears to be her son comes to greet her. The old woman's once dour face brightens.

20 Faye goes back to the Redtail, and receives a message from Spike, telling her to come back. Feigning resilience, Faye yells, "Don't assume I'm coming back! You've got to be kidding! I have a place to go back to!" and cuts off the communication!

"I have a place to go back to!"

INTERLUDE

The man who greets the old woman at the airport is Alfred, aka Punch from "BIG SHOT," which was cancelled in Session 23. His off-camera face evinces a soft concern for his mother. When director Watanabe decided to have "BIG SHOT" cancelled, the writer, Keiko Nobumoto, decided to have Punch re-appear.

SESSION#25

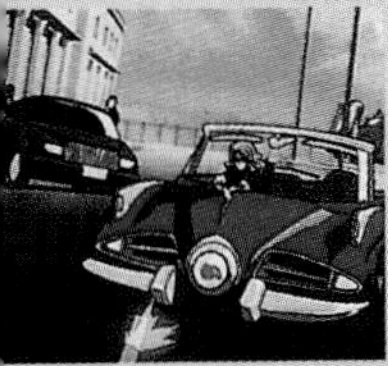
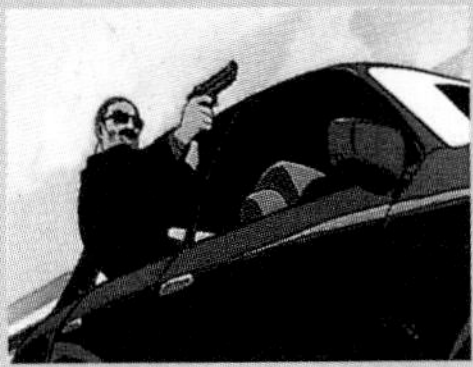

21 Angry with Spike, Faye mumbles, "What's with the attitude?" Just then, Julia's car passes by, under gunfire from men in a black car. When Faye sees this, Faye takes out her gun and shoots out the black car's tires. Julia comes back and stops in front of Faye. Their eyes meet, and Faye gets into the car, unaware who its driver really is.

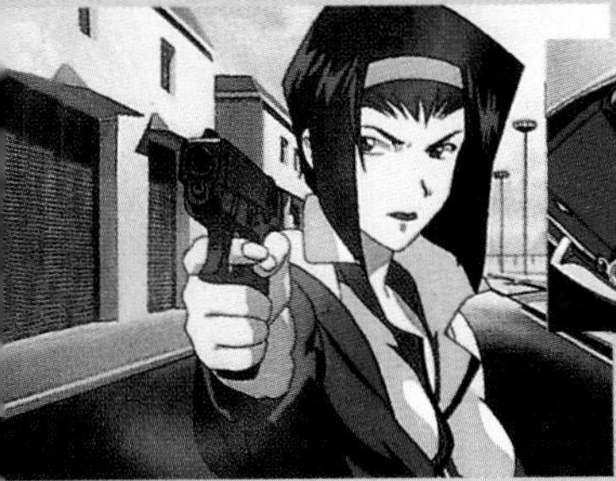
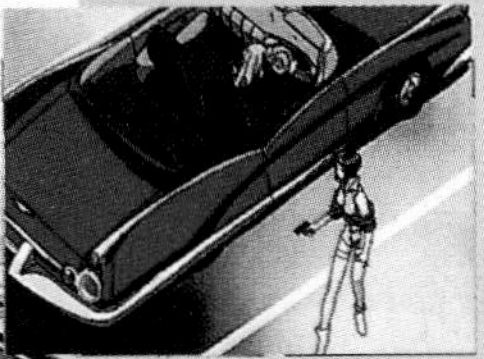
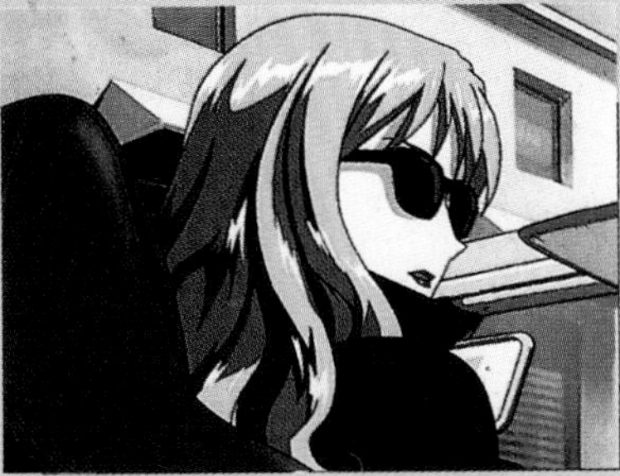
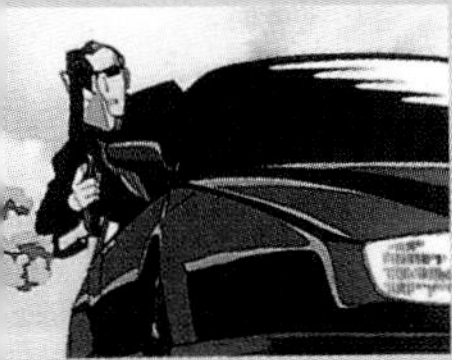
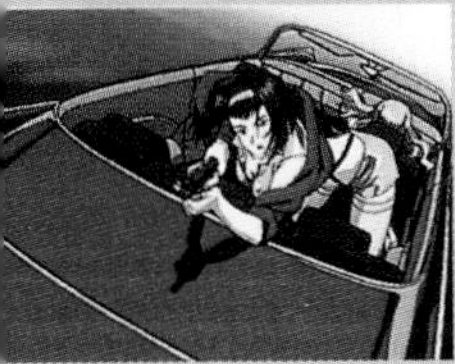
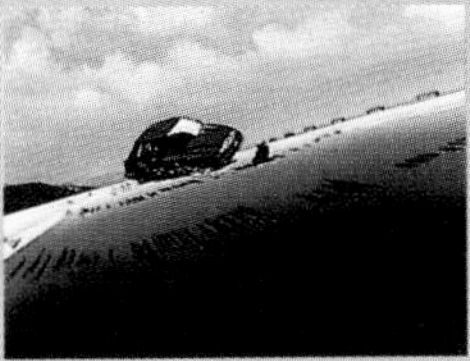

22 Soon enough, Julia and Faye are under attack by other men. The men chasing after them attack with a grenade, and Faye takes a well-aimed shot at their car. When she sees their car totaled, Faye lifts her gun and grins.

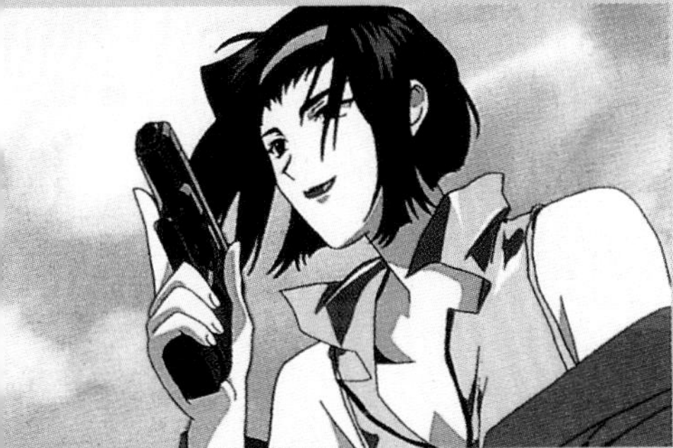
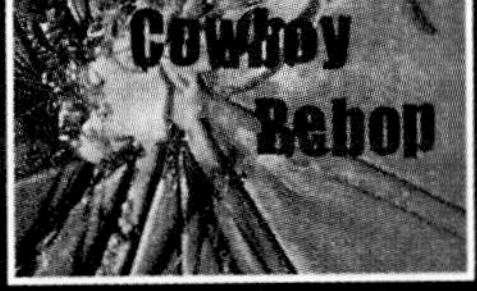
Cowboy
Bebop
EYE CATCH

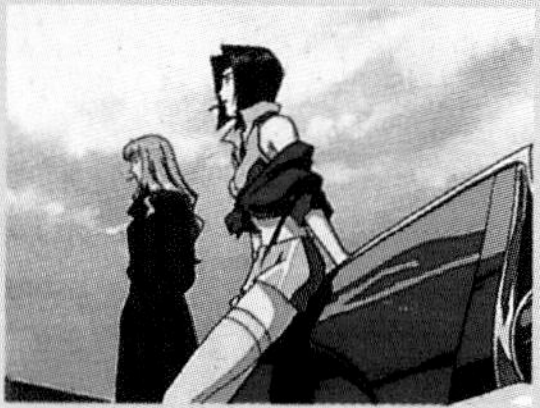

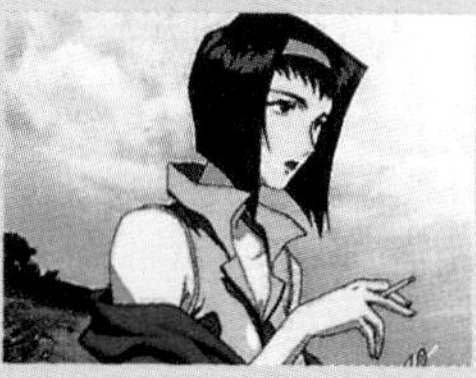

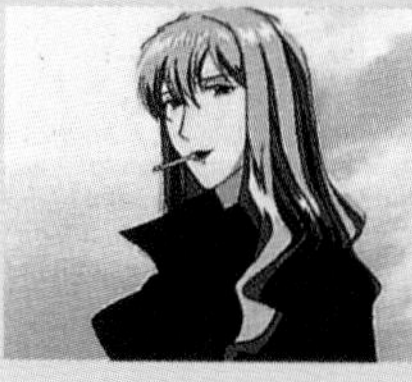

23 Julia stops the car. The two seem to get along as they talk. During the conversation, Julia finds out Faye is a bounty hunter, and tells her "I'm looking for a bounty hunter." This makes Faye a little apprehensive, but when Julia offers her a ride, she gets into the car.

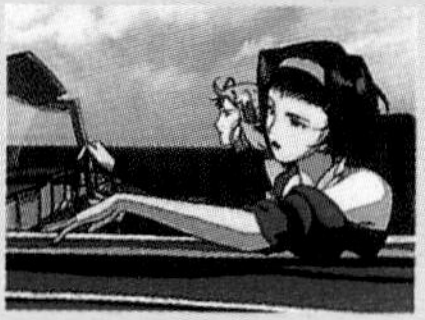

24 "What's your name?" Julia asks. Faye answers, "Faye Valentine." Julia is shocked when she hears that name. "It's a common name. What's yours?" "Julia," and then, just like Faye, "It's a common name."

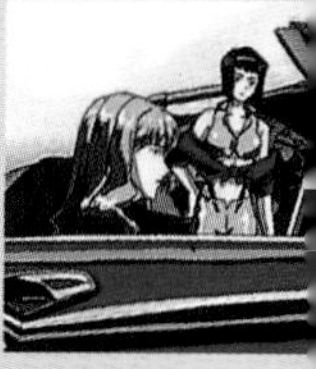

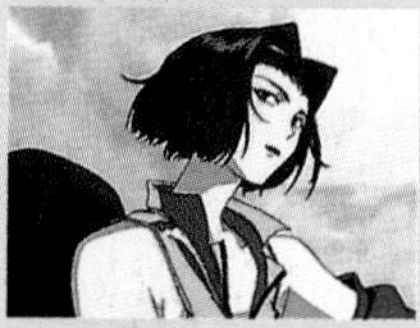

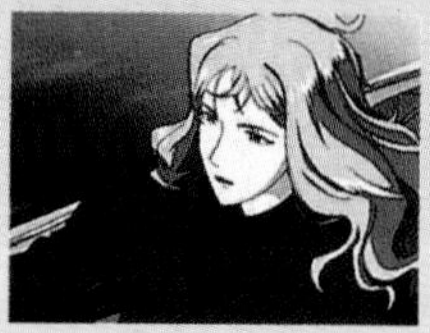

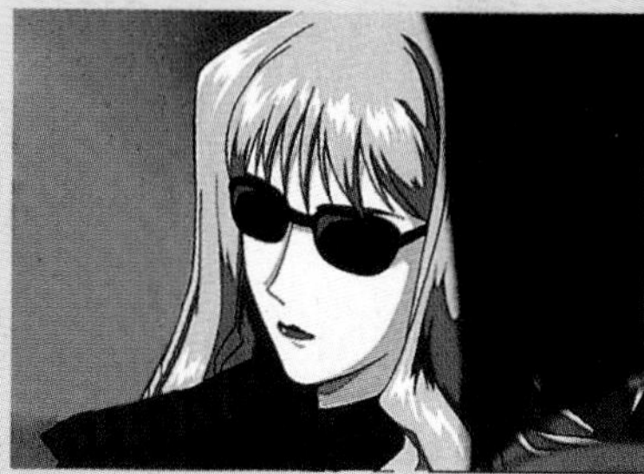

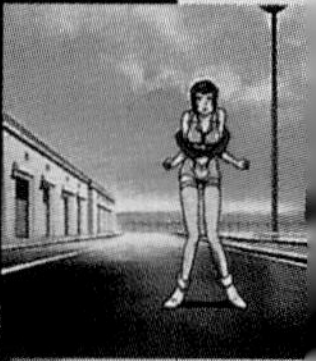

25 Julia returns Faye to the airport. Just as she is about to ask Julia about her name, Julia says "Tell Spike I'll be waiting there." Then she drives off, leaving a stunned Faye behind.

Julia's Message to Spike…

Faye helps out Julia, without even realizing who she is. Completely blind to the other's identity, the two hit it off, perhaps a mutual taste of danger draws them together. But when they part ways, Julia leaves a message for Spike: "I'll be waiting there." When Faye hears this, she realizes that this is Spike's Julia. Meanwhile, Spike and Jet head for Tharsis in the Bebop. Jet warns Spike not to be a slave to the past. Faye returns. She tells Spike that she saw Julia. But just then, the ship comes under attack. A Red Dragon fighter followed Faye. As Spike starts to coordinate a counter-attack, Faye tells him Julia's message. He looks surprised for a moment, and then leaves to attack. Meanwhile at the Red Dragon headquarters, Vicious' punishment, is about to begin!

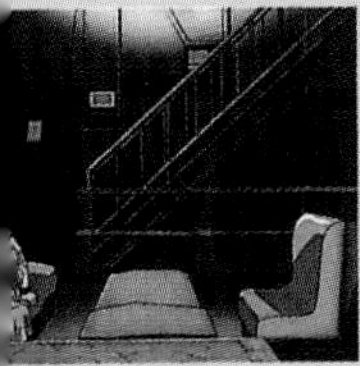

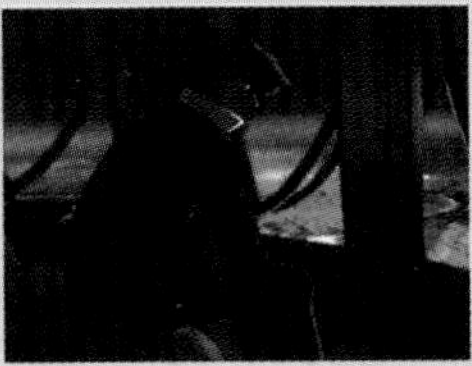

SESSION#25

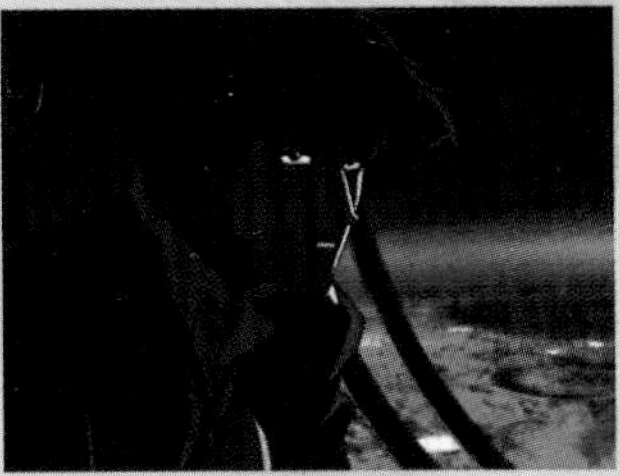

?6 The Bebop heads for Tharsis. Jets tells a fable ›f a man who got too wrapped up in the past. "I ıate that story," he concludes and asks Spike to Turn back." "When we first met, you said, 'I've ılready died once.' So don't go resurrecting your-elf."

'7 Spike doesn't answer ím, and begins talking ɔout Julia. "When I saw ılia for the first time, I saw woman who was truly live. She is a piece of me ıat I've lost. My other half ve been longing for." Jet is urprised that Spike would ven start talking about Julia n his own.

"For the first time, I saw a woman who was truly alive."

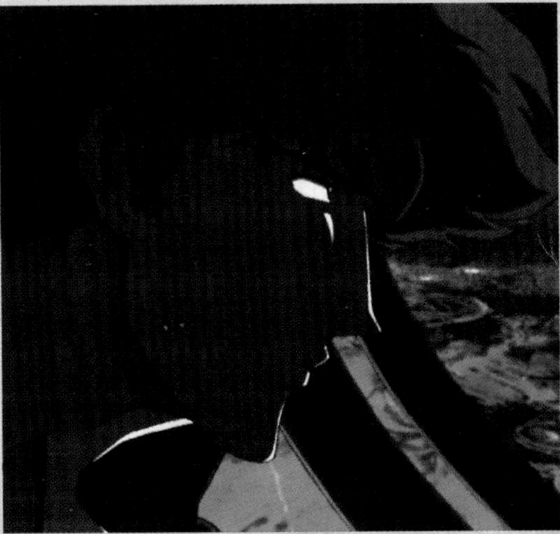

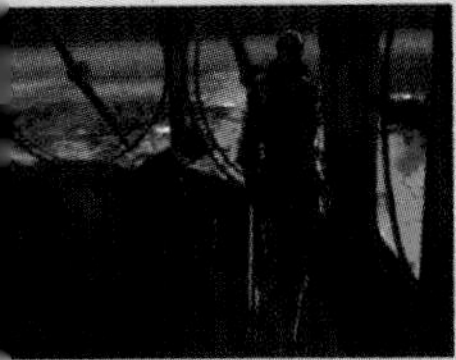

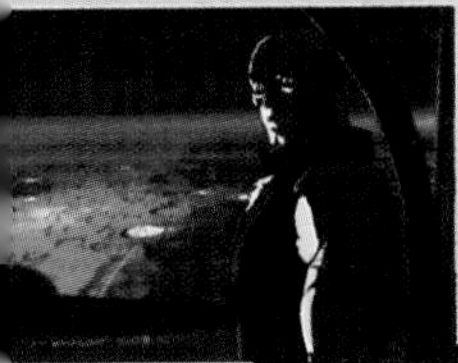

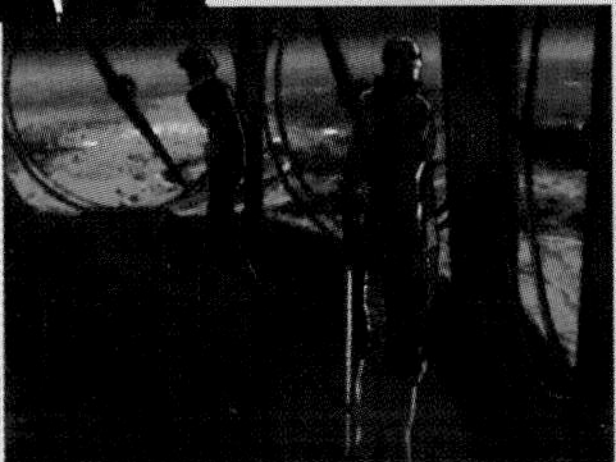

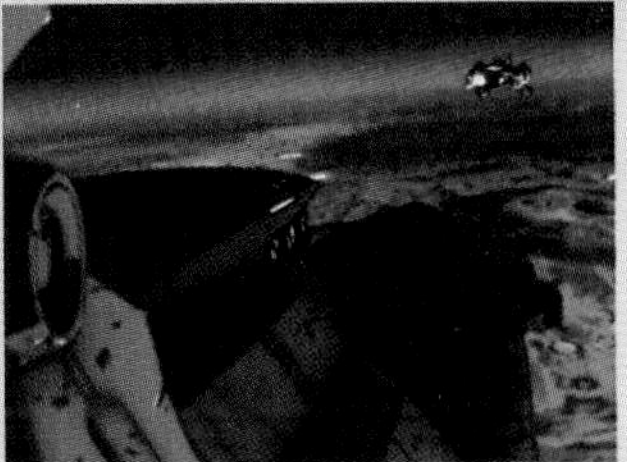

28 Jet resigns himself to the fact that he won't persuade Spike to let it go. "She's back." Jet asks, "Huh? Who?" and looks outside the bridge, where he sees Faye's Redtail drawing up to the Bebop.

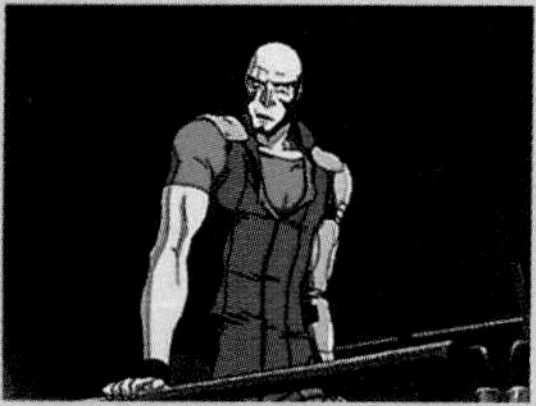

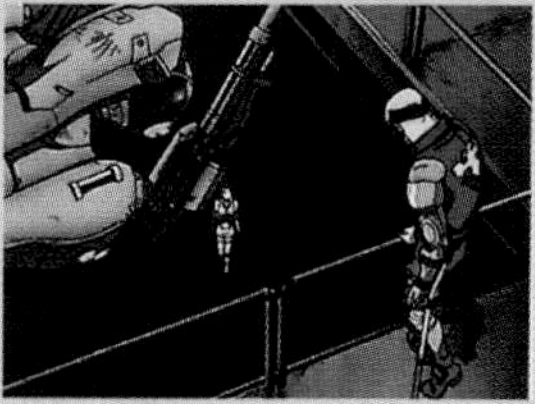

29 Jet takes one look at the battle-torn Redtail and says, "This isn't a repair shop!" Faye ignores his comment and asks, "The guy with the fluffy hair here? I'm delivering a message. From Julia." Jet is shocked to hear that name!

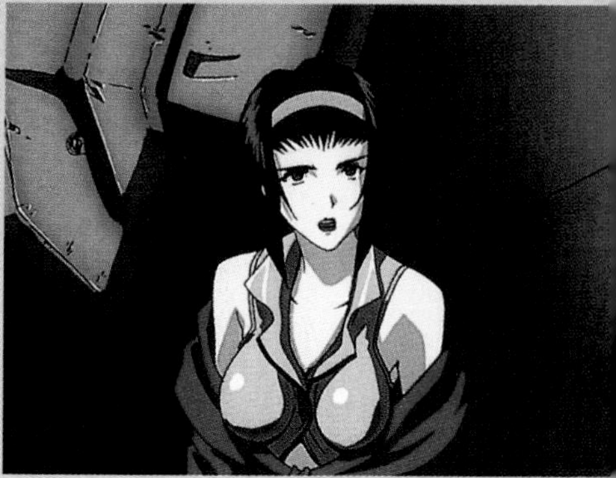

INTERLUDE

Julia encounters Faye as she's being chased by Red Dragon flunkies. It may look like Julia had planned this meeting, but it was total coincidence, and, as it turns out, serendipitous. Julia had heard Faye's name from Shin.

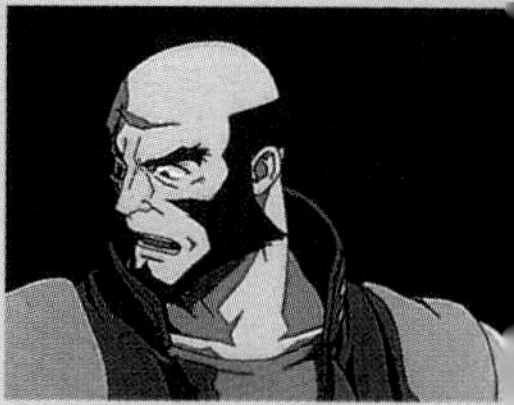

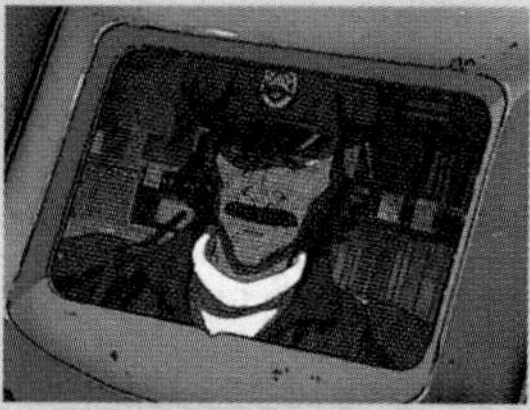

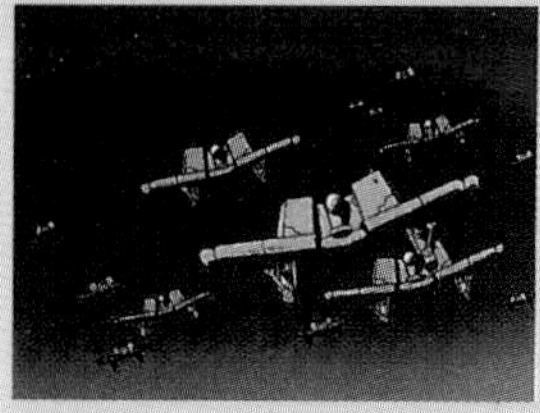

"...Too late for that."

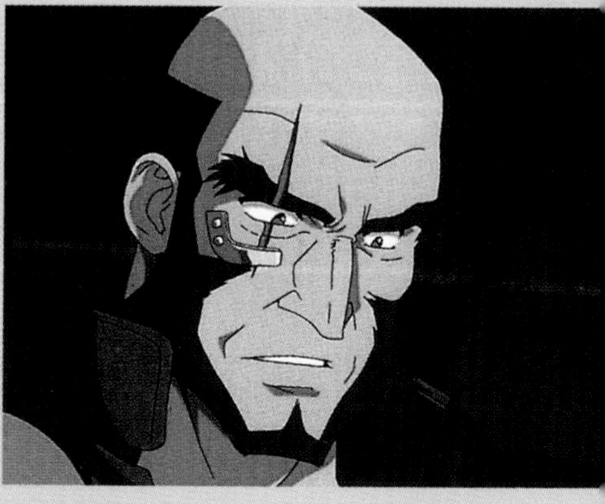

30 Bob, a buddy from the police force, calls Jet to tell him about the infighting in the Red Dragons. The elders are going after everyone associated with Vicious, including those who have left the syndicate entirely. Bob warns Jet to leave Mars, but it's too late.

SESSION#25

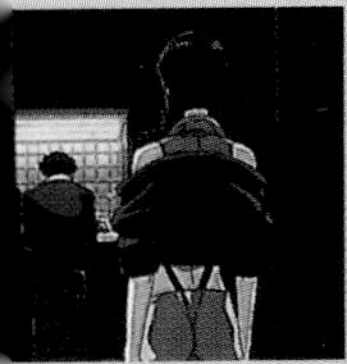

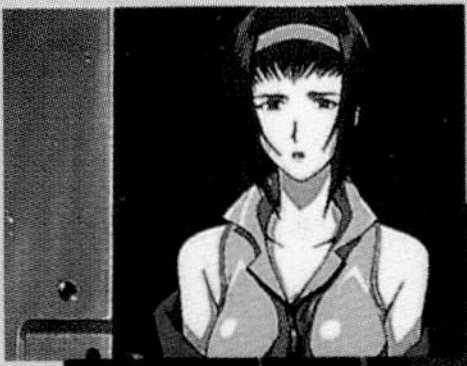

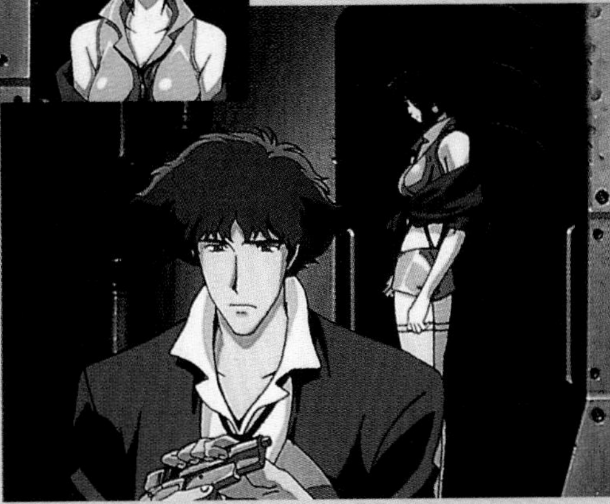

1 Faye approaches ›ike, but she can't ›eak. When she turns to ›ave, Spike asks her, ›What is it? You look like ›u have information." ›e tries to act tough and ›ys, "How much will you ›y for it?"

'You look like you ›ave information."
"How much will you pay for it?"

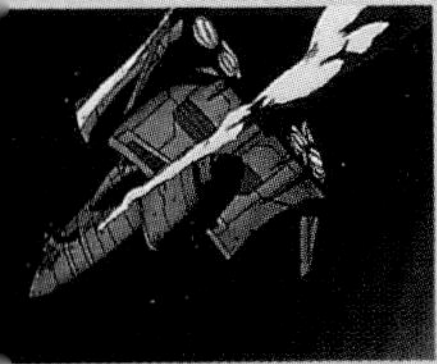

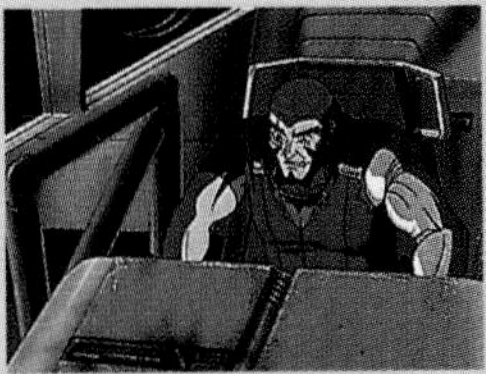

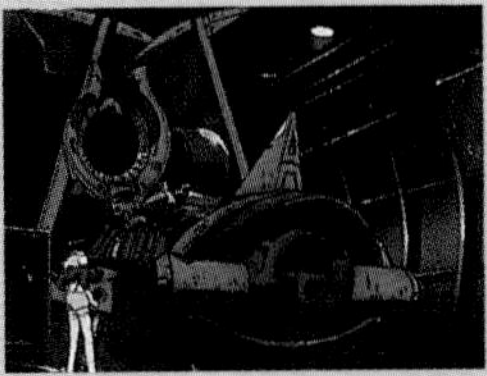

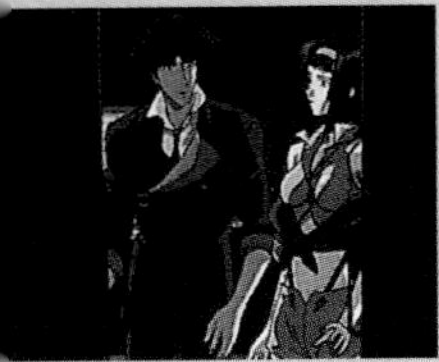

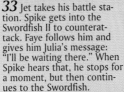

33 Jet takes his battle station. Spike gets into the Swordfish II to counterattack. Faye follows him and gives him Julia's message: "I'll be waiting there." When Spike hears that, he stops for a moment, but then continues to the Swordfish.

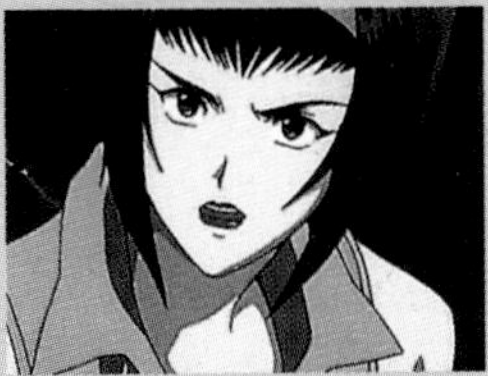

'2 Just then, the ship ›kes a hit. Spike asks ›ye, "Were you fol-›wed?" Faye is surprised, ›t Spike says, "Well, it ›as bound to happen ›oner or later."

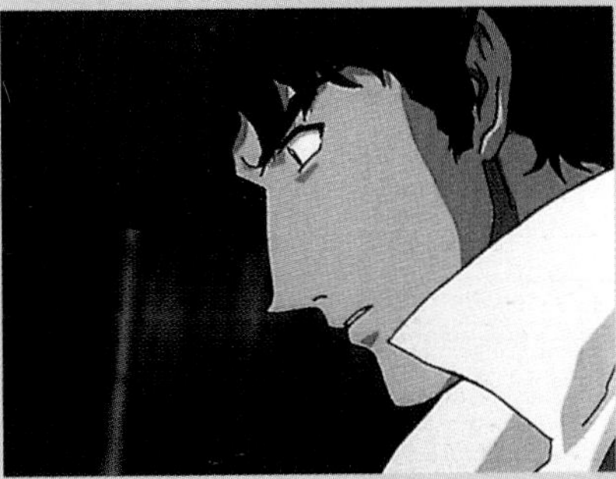

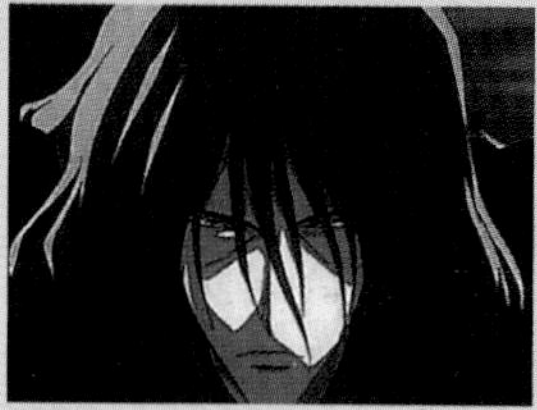

34 The judgment room. The elders declare Vicious' punishment. "You who have caused a disturbance in the clan. By the will of the clan, you shall be executed." They ask him if he has any last words. "No."

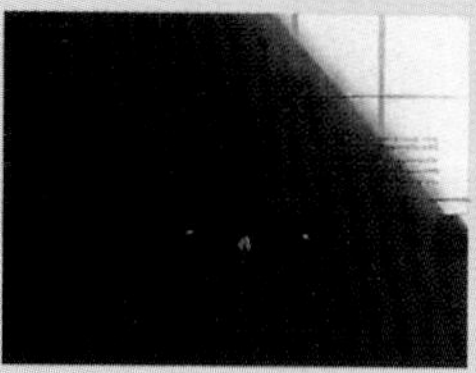

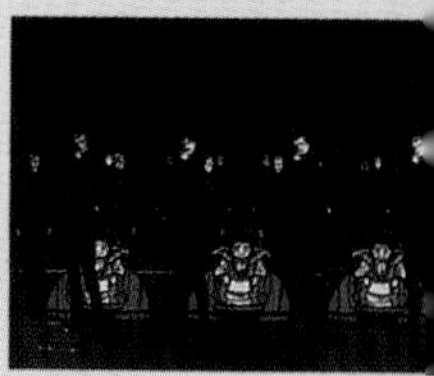

INTERLUDE

The story Jet tells Spike in this session, about the man who was wounded in the leg while hunting, is from "The Snows of Kilimanjaro," by the American author Ernest Hemingway. And, the story Spike tells Jet, of the cat who lived and died a million times, is an allusion to the picture book "The Cat With a Million Lives" by Youko Sano.

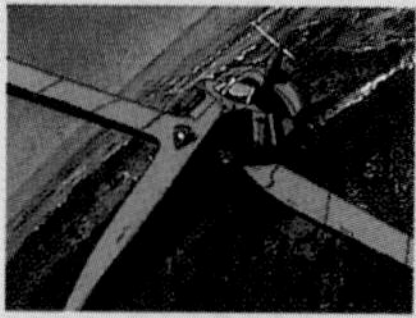

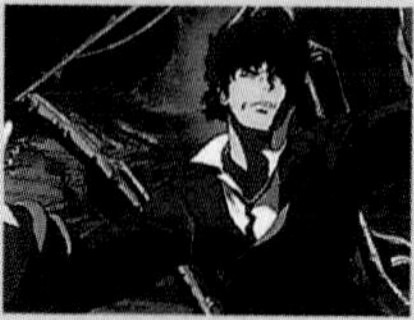

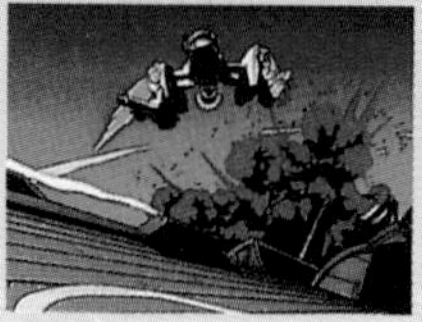

35 Red Dragon fighters attack the Bebop. Spike gets into an intense dogfight with the enemy. Faye goes on the attack too in the Redtail, even though it hasn't been repaired!

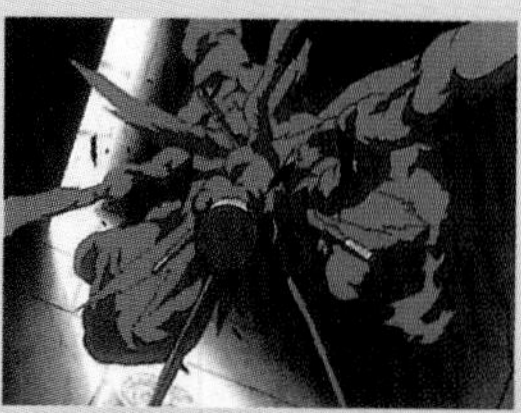

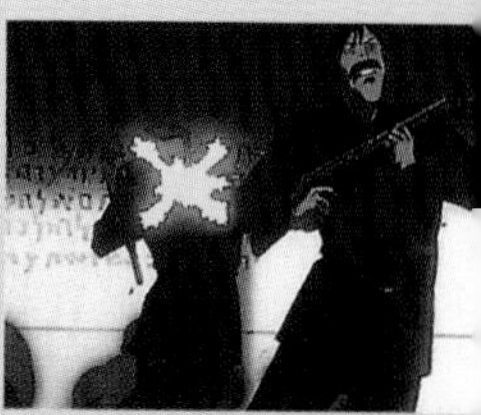

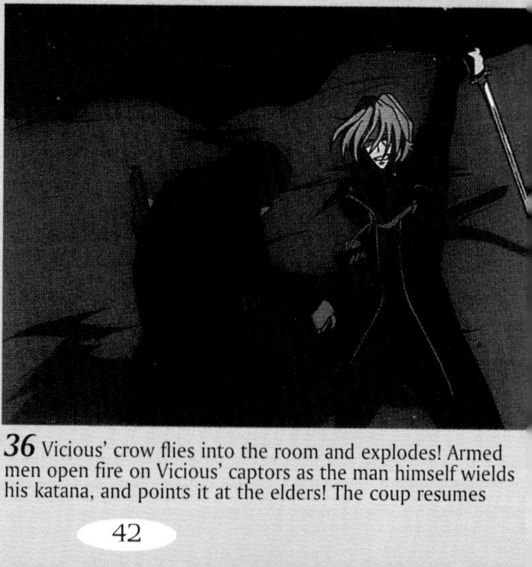

36 Vicious' crow flies into the room and explodes! Armed men open fire on Vicious' captors as the man himself wields his katana, and points it at the elders! The coup resumes

SESSION#25

37 The judgment room is in chaos. Vicious walks up to Wang Long and grins. "You shall shed red tears." Vicious slices with his katana, and rivers of red blood pour out of Wang Long.

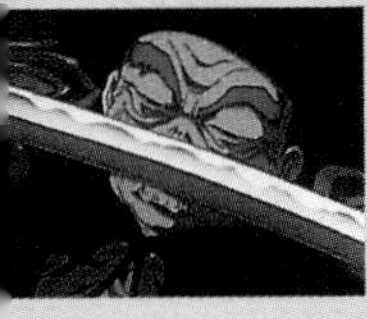

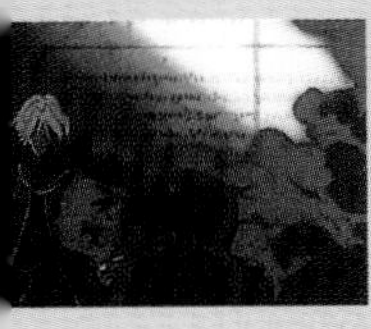

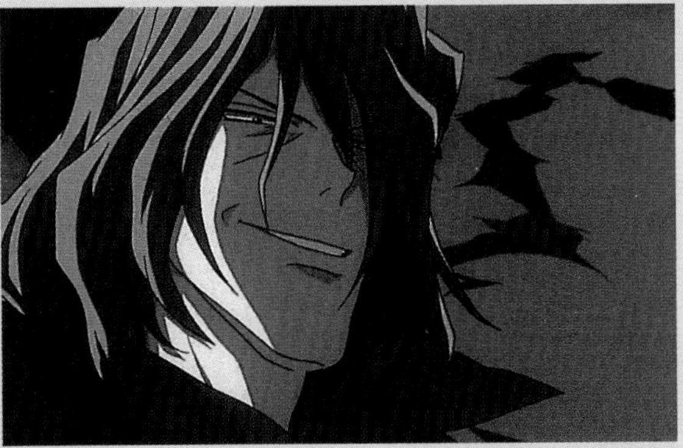

"You shall shed red tears."

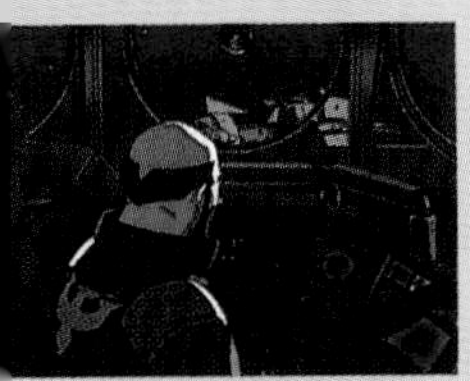

38 Spike and Faye have a tough time against the enemy. But in the midst of battle, Jet calls Spike on the communicator and tells him, "We've got things covered here, so go. Go, regain what you lost." Jet's words push Spike, who had been hesitating about whether to find Julia!

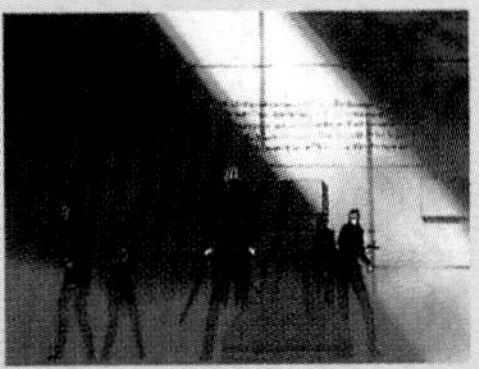

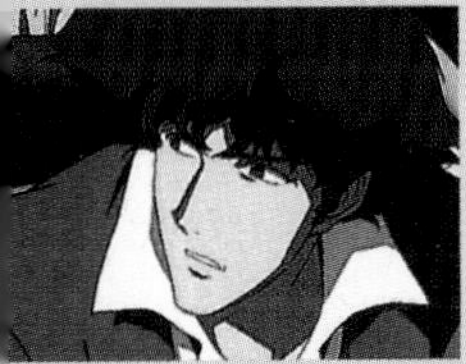

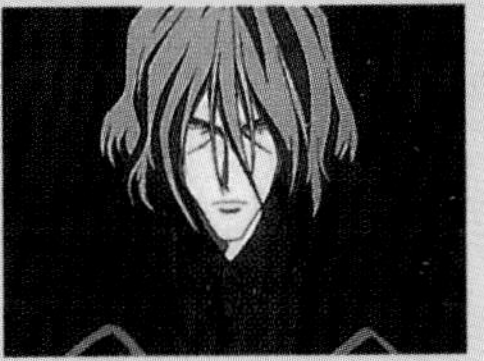

39 Vicious sheaths his katana. He proclaims victory. "As of now, the leadership has changed hands. I now command the authority of this syndicate!!"

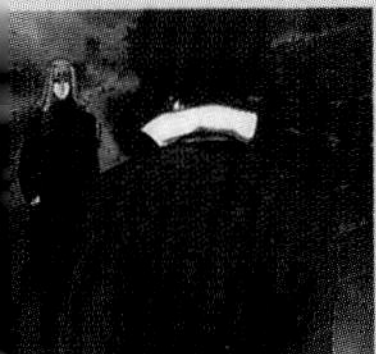

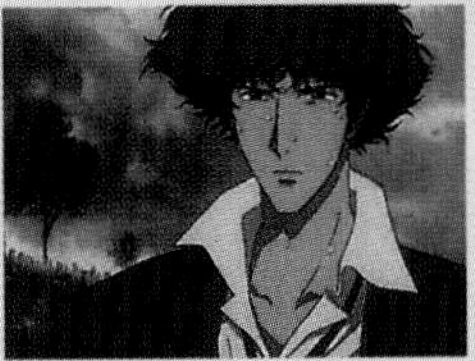

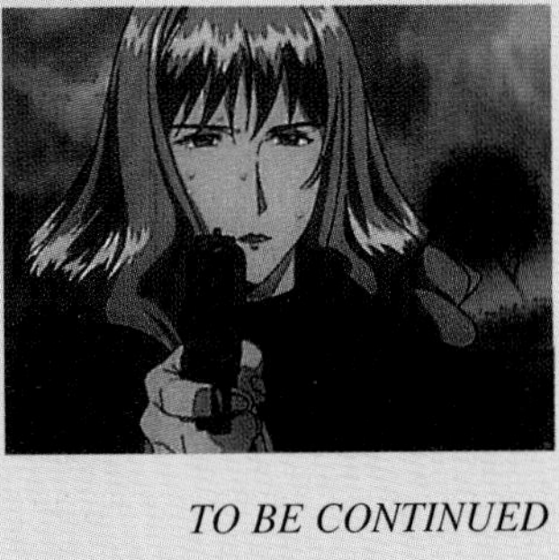

40 Rain falls on a graveyard at the edge of town, just like it did on that day Spike and Julia parted. Spike returns and is reunited with Julia ... but aiming a gun at him.

TO BE CONTINUED

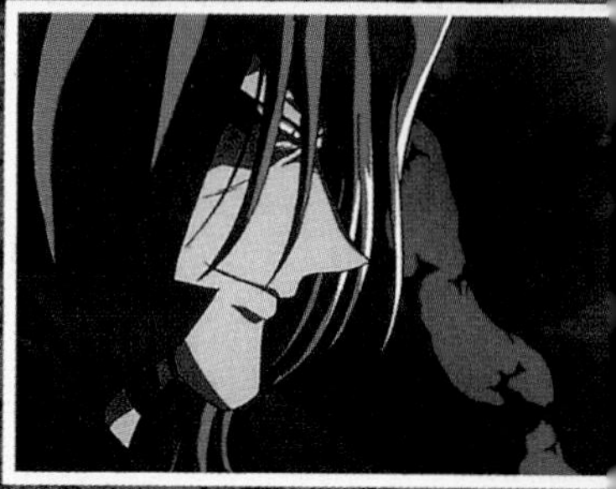

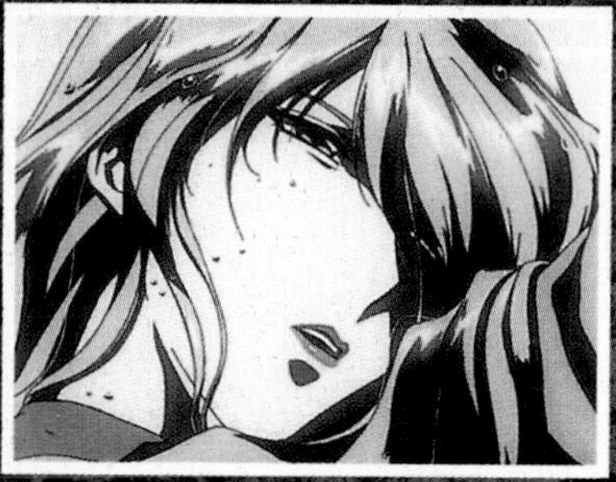

The Real Fol

After a long time apart, Spike and Julia reunite. But their happiness is short-lived at best. That which Spike has longed for slips through his fingers as easily as it came into his embrace. This is one man's fate, converging unto death as it were a predestined circumstance of his young life. Having lost his future, Spike is left only with his past. He confronts Vicious in a battle that should have taken place long ago. What does that right eye, left in a wounded body, see at the very end?

Session#26

ザ・リアル・フォークブルース
〈後編〉

SESSION#26

Scenario : Keiko Nobumoto
Continuity : Shinichirou Watanabe
Director : Yoshiyuki Takei

blues (Part 2)

1 As Julia draws closer to Spike - her gun aimed squarely at him - she begins to speak quietly. "It was raining on that day too…" "Is that why you didn't come? Because of the rain?" Spike smiles. Julia reveals the truth: "I was supposed to kill you…"

2 "That day…If I had killed you, I would have been free." The past replays in Julia's mind. Spike gazes at her. "Why didn't you do it?" Julia doesn't answer, but asks instead, "Why did you love me?"

Spike and Julia are finally brought together

Spike and Julia's reunion is punctuated by Vicious, having seized the power of the syndicate, sending men to hunt them down. In order to hide from those men, they visit Annie's shop. However, they find Annie mortally wounded. But Annie dies relieved to know that the two were able to meet again. After staying with her until her death, Spike leaves the shop, armed to the teeth, to begin preparations for battle.

In the meantime, Jet and Faye manage to beat back the enemy, but not without enormous damage to both their ships. Worried about Spike, Jet visits the fortune-teller Laughing Bull to find out where he is.

Spike and Julia fight with Vicious' subordinates. They make a perfect team, and together they are able to escape from Annie's shop. But the moment Julia lets her guard down, a single bullet pierces her body!

SESSION#26

3 Held in Spike's arms, Julia reiterates what Spike had said on that day: "Let's run away somewhere, just like this. Really escape from this world, somewhere with no one else around, just the two of us." For a moment, the two of them cross over time to return to that day...

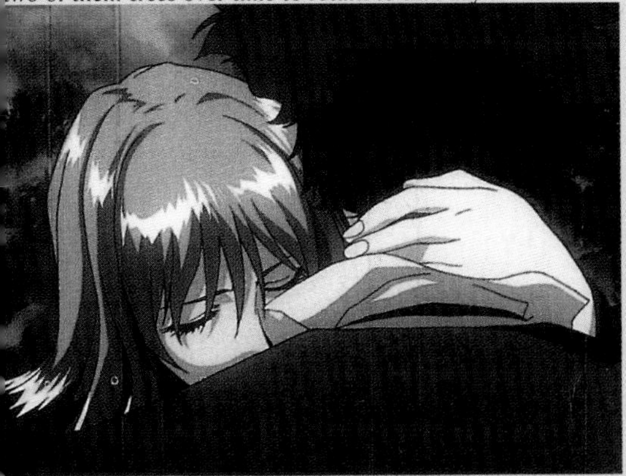

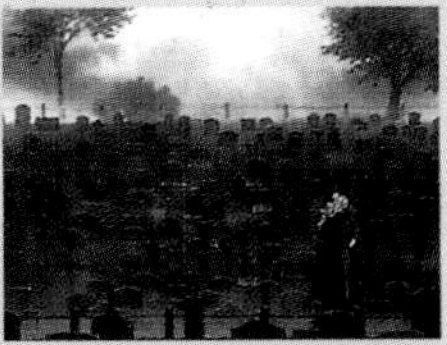

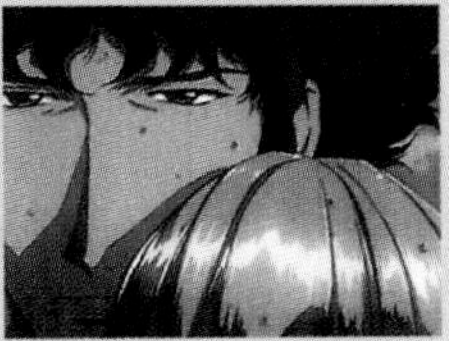

"Let's run away, just like this."

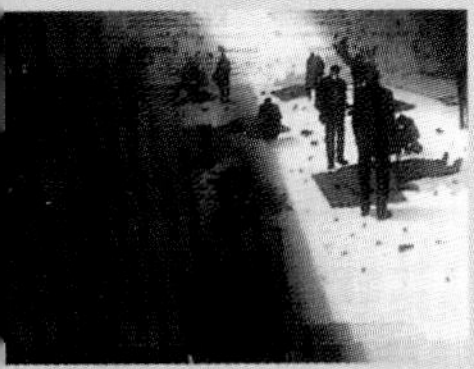

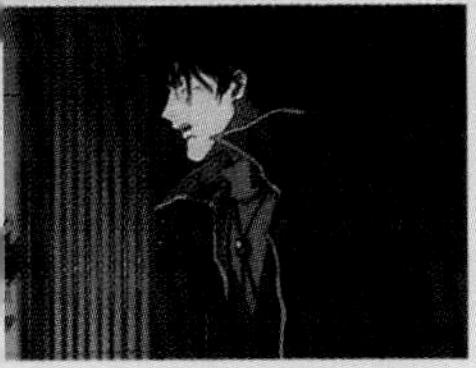

4 Shin returns to the Red Dragon Headquarters and steps into a judgment room riddled with bullets, littered with dead bodies, and painted with blood. Vicious walks up from behind the dumbfounded Shin and explains how things went down in his absence.

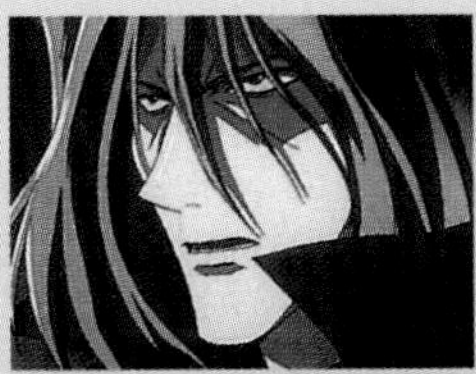

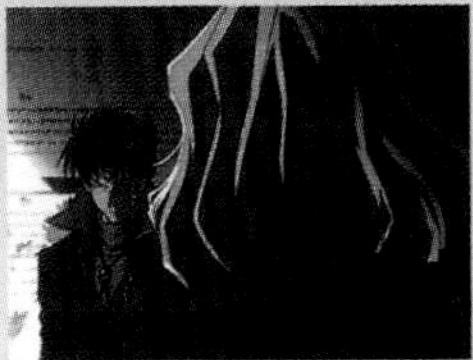

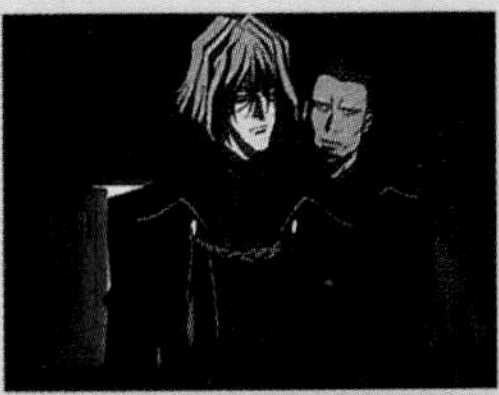

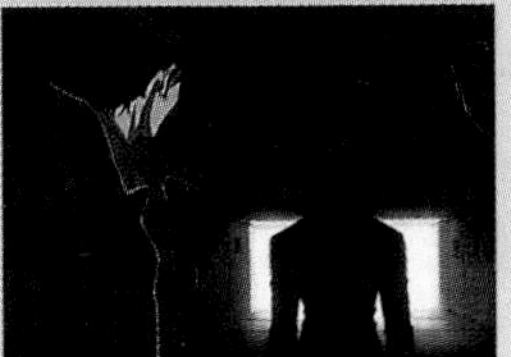

5 Vicious asks, "What happened to him?" Shin makes the shameful excuse, "......He got away," and freezes to avoid Vicious' piercing look. "Don't make the same mistake as Lin," Vicious says as he turns to leave.

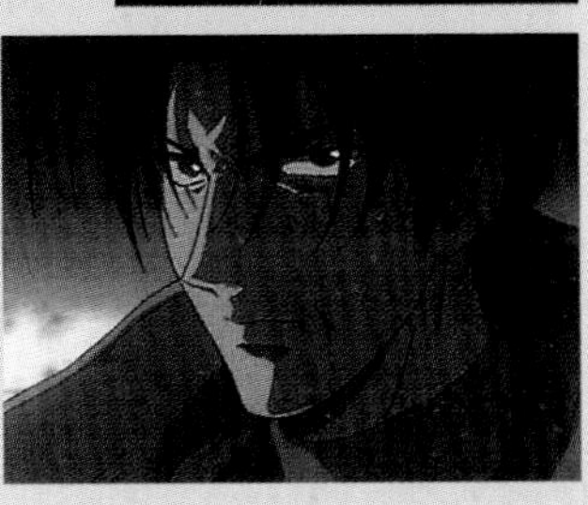

6 Spike and Julia go to Annie's shop, which Spike admits may already be surrounded by Red Dragon minions. Spike enters to find Annie cradling a gunshot wound to the stomach. "I told them you weren't here. Said you were already dead.."

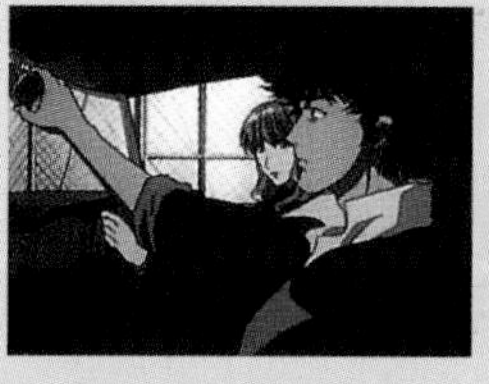

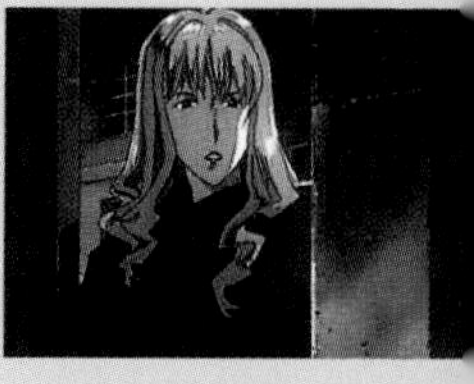

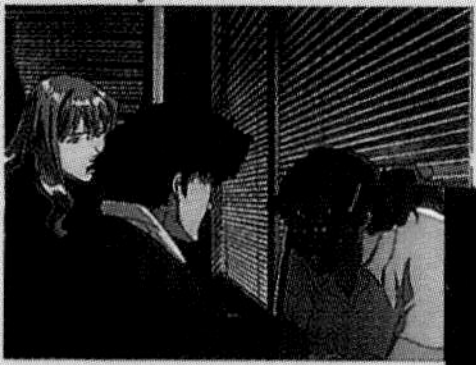

"It's...unusually cold today, isn't it..."

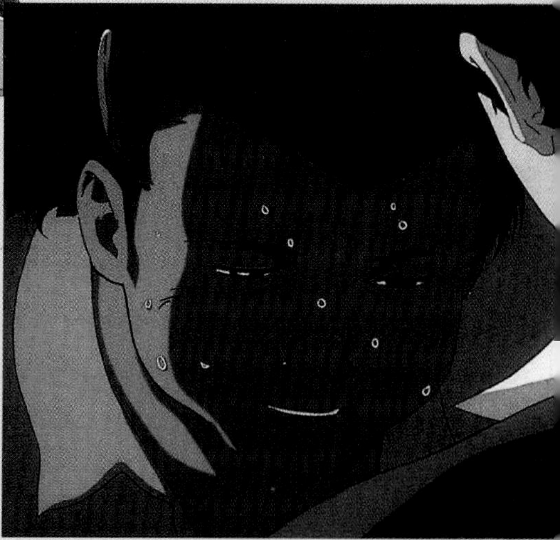

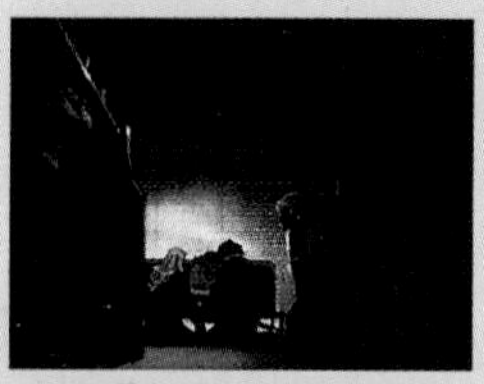

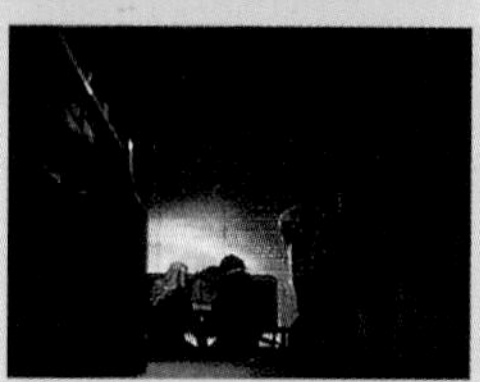

7 Spike tells Annie not to speak and puts pressure on her wound. Annie tells Spike that Vicious has killed the elders. When she sees Julia, she says, "You were able to find Julia...I'm glad." A satisfied smile spreads across Annie's face as she dies.

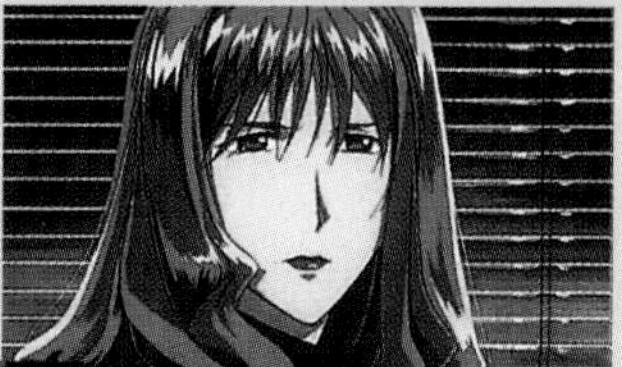

8 Spike leaves the shop, taking weapons with him, to begin preparations for a final showdown. "You don't need those kinds of things just to run away somewhere," Julia says. She resigns herself to the fact that Spike is going to confront Vicious, and decides that she will stay with him to the end.

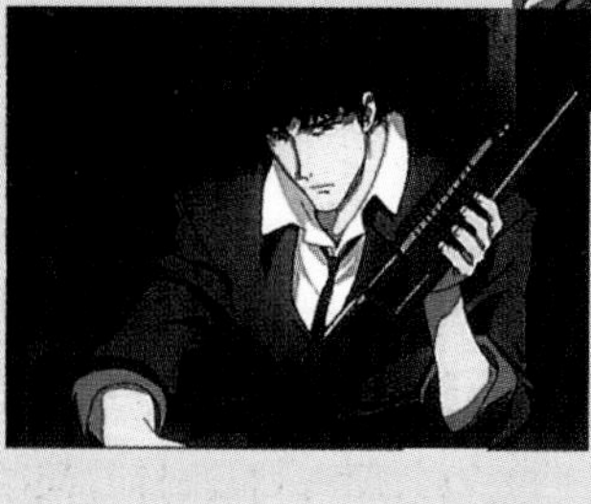

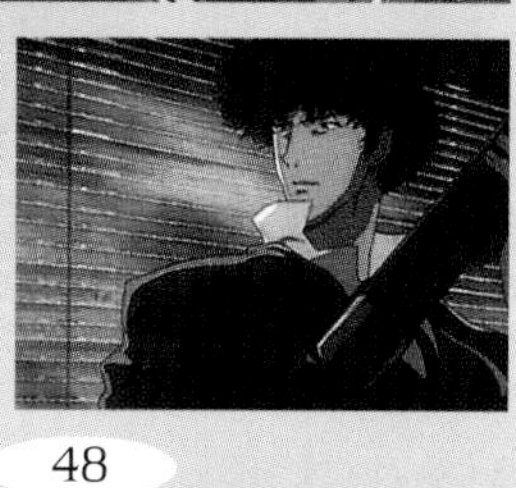

SESSION#26

9 The Bebop, damanged from the assault, crash lands in the wilderness. As Jet works intently on repairing the ship, aye probes him about his feelings for Spike. He's not coming back, you know? He probably got killed somewhere." "Probably."

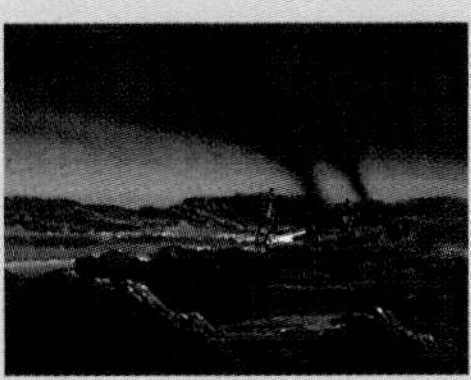

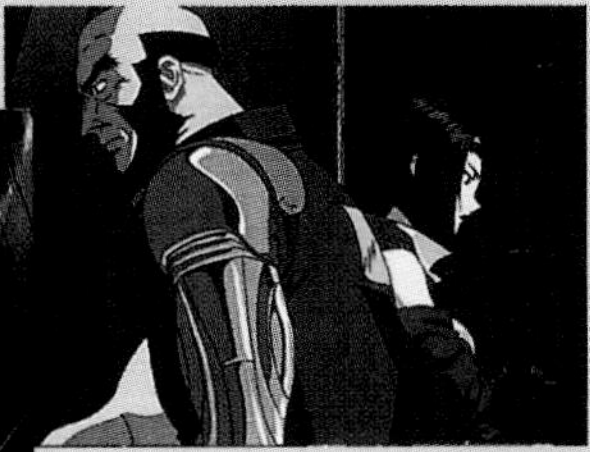

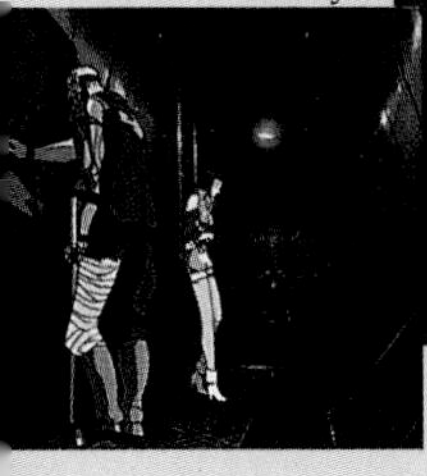

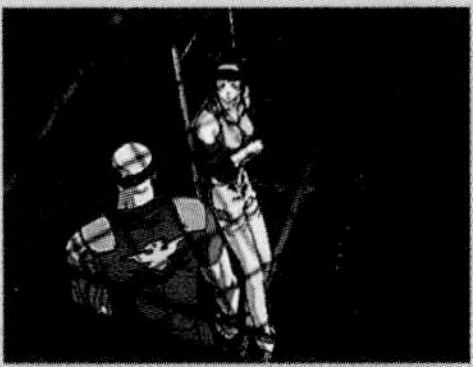

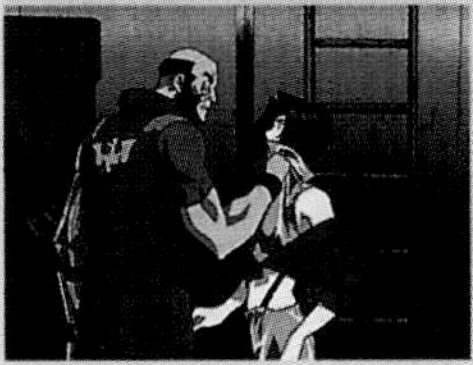

10 "So what about it?" Jet shouts. "You want me to go looking for him? You gotta be kidding! He left to deal with his past." "You made him go," Faye fires back. Jet grabs Faye by the collar and yells out, "My leg is wounded, my ship is ruined! That's right! He was nothin' but trouble! Like I care!"

INTERLUDE

This session skips the opening credits, and cuts right to the first frame of the story. This is quite unusual for an animated TV series. This sets it apart from other sessions and makes it distinctive.

"A demonic angel…
Or maybe an angelic demon…"

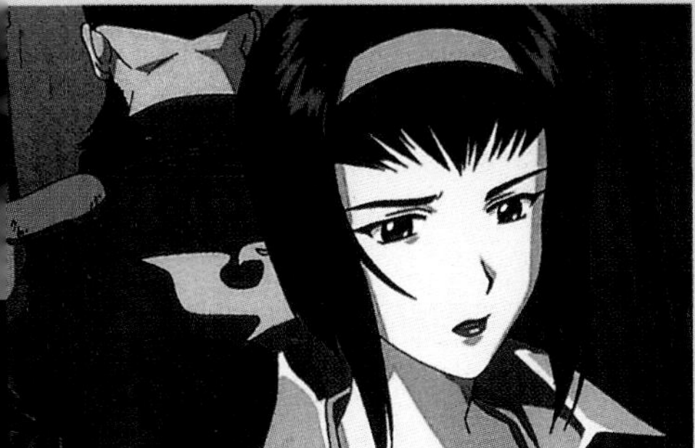

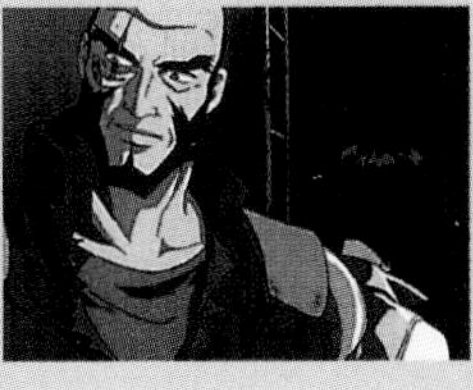

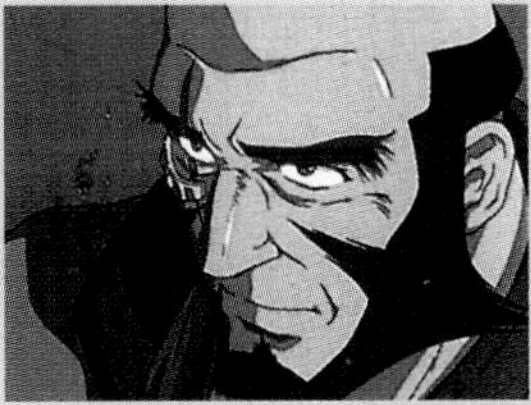

11 But, Jet is worried about Spike after all, and asks about Julia. "She's a woman. A beautiful, dangerous, woman. "A demonic angel… or maybe an angelic demon…"

12 Julia's car explodes, signaling an enslaught of Vicious' subordinates to storm Annie's store, guns ablaze. As Julia leads him up some stairs, Spike returns the enemy fire.

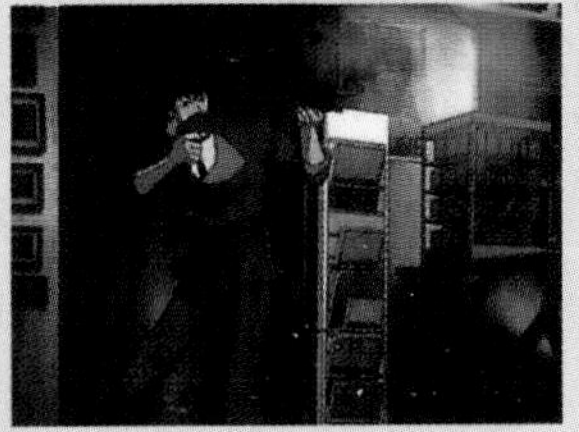

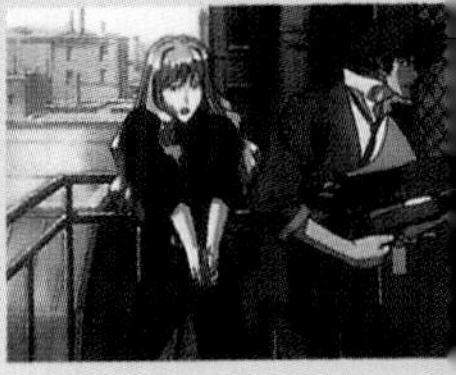

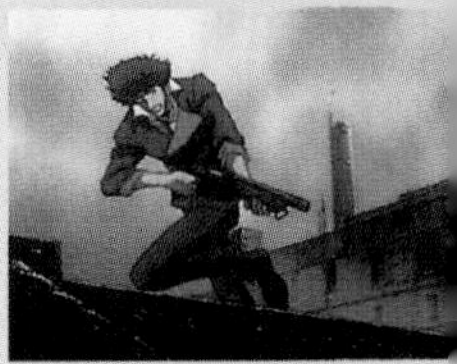

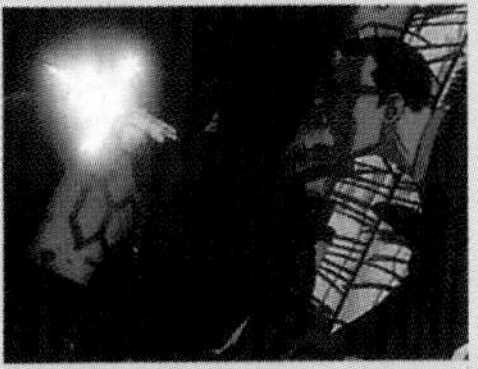

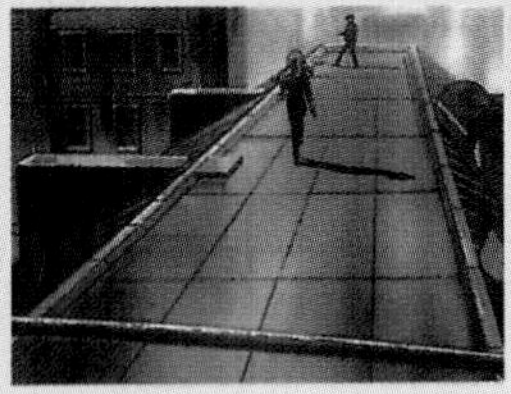

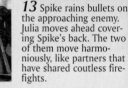

13 Spike rains bullets on the approaching enemy. Julia moves ahead covering Spike's back. The two of them move harmoniously, like partners that have shared coutless firefights.

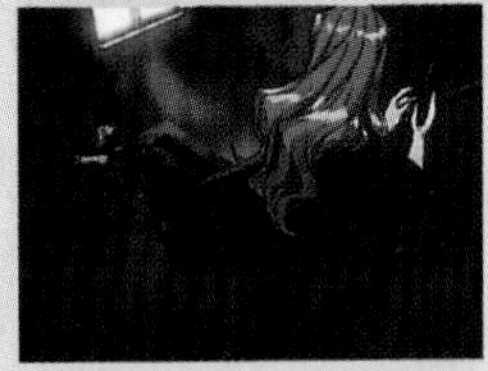

INTERLUDE

The song that plays as Spike invades the Red Dragon building in the second half of this episode, is "See You Space Cowboys," a different arrangement on the ending theme (and available on the 3rd OST). Originally, the director, Watanabe, liked it so much, he actually wanted to use this version as the ending theme. However, because of various circumstances, this arrangement wasn't used until the final episode.

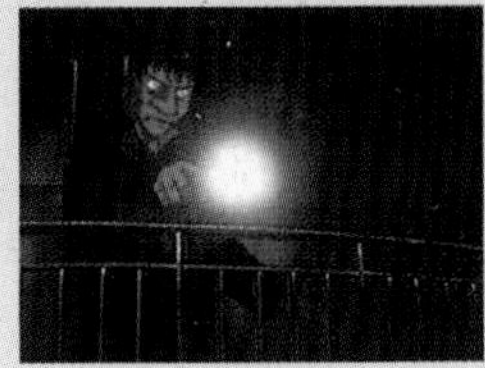

14 They're ambushed on the roof. Spike strikes down enemies with quick efficiency, convinced he's nailed them all. But a hidden thug fires a bullet into Julia's back! Spike instinctively strikes back, killing the gunman. But Julia collapses before him…

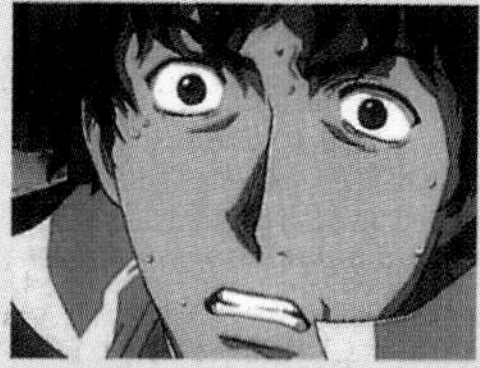

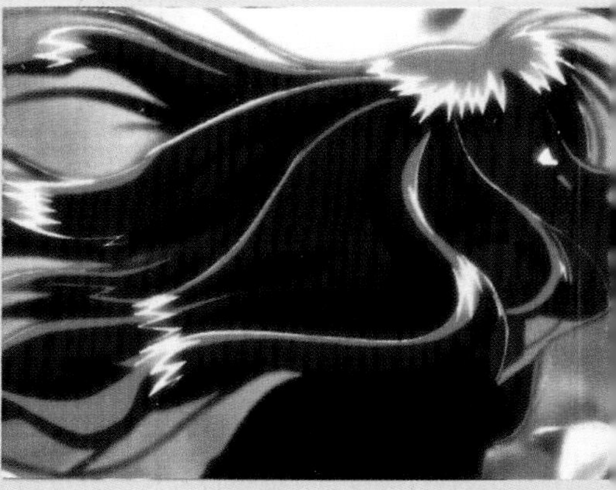

SESSION#26

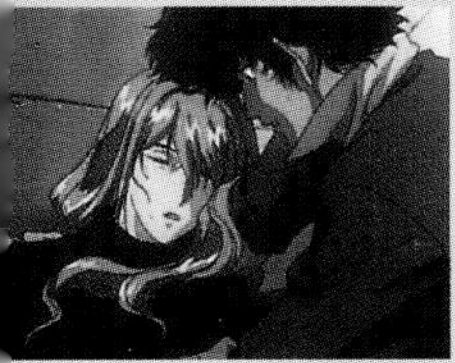

15 Spike tosses his gun away and rushes to Julia's side. As he holds her, Julia moves her lips faintly, desperate trying to speak. There in Spike's arms, Julia slips into death.

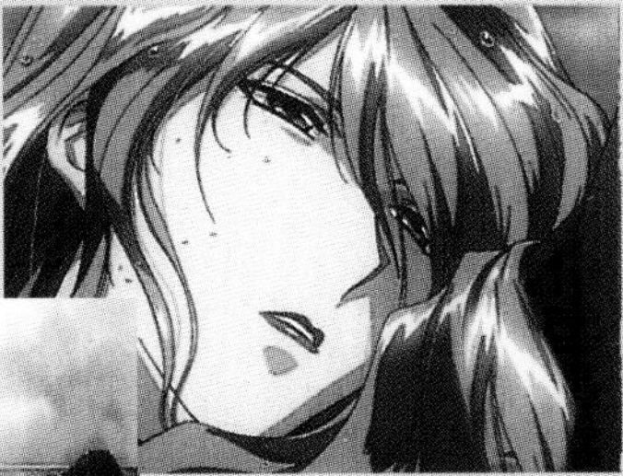

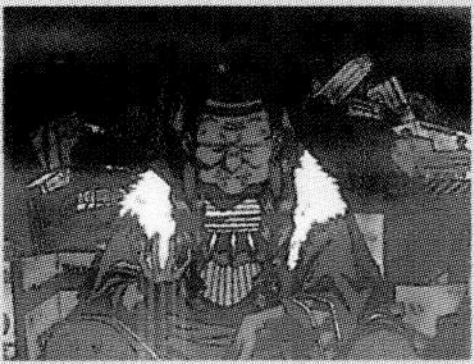

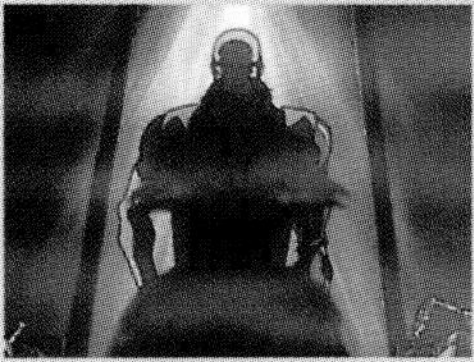

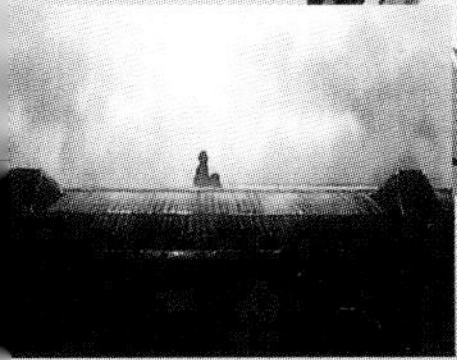

16 Jet visits the fortune teller Laughing Bull to find out where Spike is. Bull tells Jet that all living things have their own star. "The moment a life is born, a star is born also. It becomes a guardian star. When a life has run out, the star too falls and disappears." Jet looks away and says, "Don't say that."

"Do not fear death. Death is always with you."

17 Bull calls out to Jet, "Running Rock! His star is going to fall." Jet refutes that. Bull tells him quietly, "Do not be afraid of death. Death is always with you. The moment you show fear, it will pounce on you faster than light. If you do not show fear, it will gently watch over you."

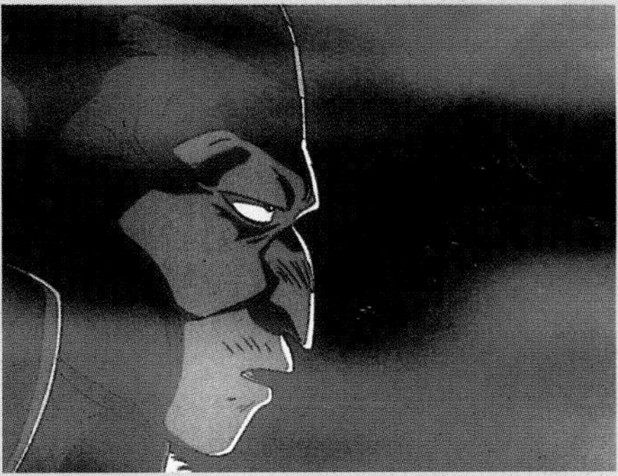

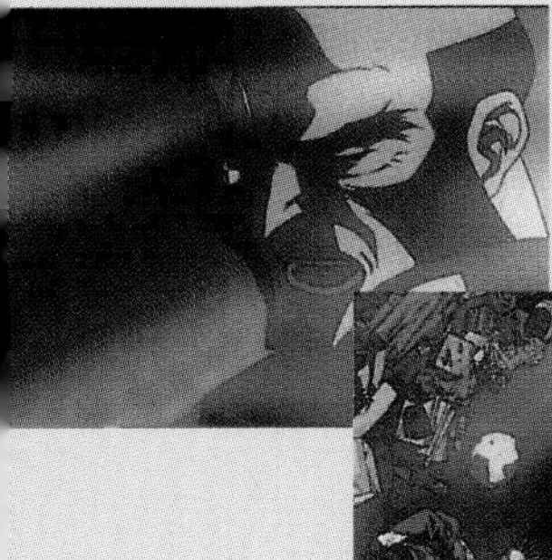

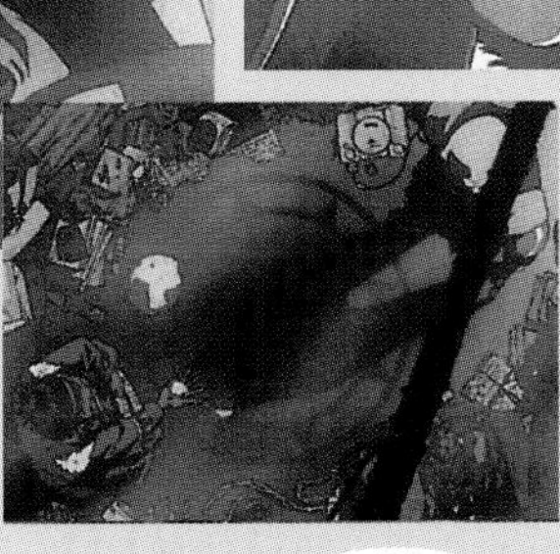

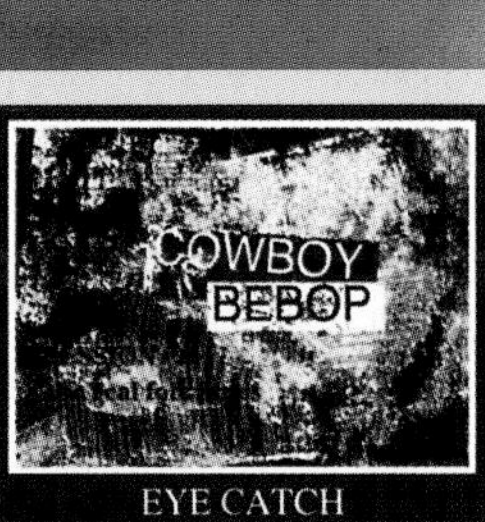
COWBOY
BEBOP
EYE CATCH

18 Vicious finds Annie's store, completely destroyed. A subordinate brings him Julia's clothes and passport. "He has nowhere to go anymore. ......He will come."

"A beast that has lost its place to go."

19 A sleeping Jet rolls over from his position on the sofa to see Spike standing there as calm as ever. Spike asks if there is anything to eat. "I'm starving."

Spike and Vicious – Two old enemies face off

Vicious visits Annie's shop and finds some things that Julia left behind. Looking at them, Vicious is confident Spike will come to confront him. Spike returns to the Bebop, much to Jet's surprise, and asks his partner to make him some food... some of his special beef with bell peppers. After the meal, Spike leaves again. Jet understands that Spike was actually saying goodbye. Faye aims her gun at Spike demanding that he not go face Vicious. But Spike explains that if doesn't go, he'll never know whether he's truly alive.

Spike invades the Red Dragon headquarters alone. He climbs to the top floor as directed by Shin, and faces off with Vicious. For these two old enemies, the time to settle their fight has come!

SESSION#26

20 Spike eats the meatless bell peppers and beef that Jet made in silence. Finally he says, "The food you make tastes as horrible as ever." "You sure seem to be eating a lot." "Well, they say hunger is the best spice." Out of the blue, Spike starts telling a story about a cat. A story about a cat who lived, died, and was reborn over and over again, then finally found true love, and died for good.

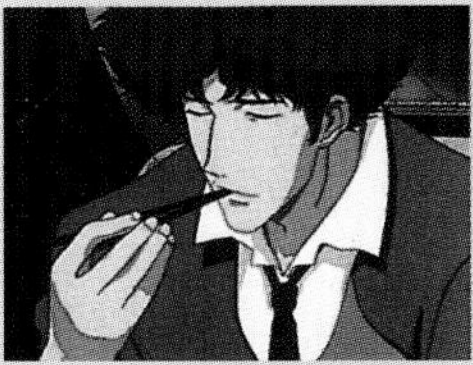

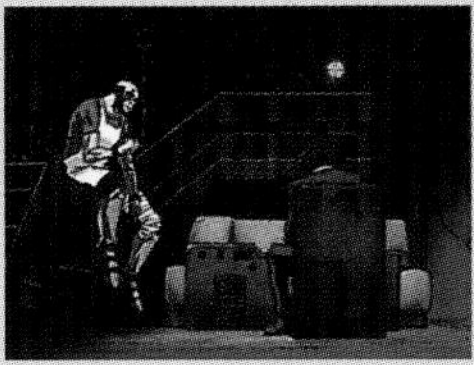

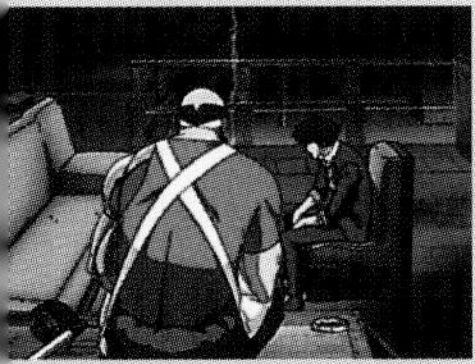

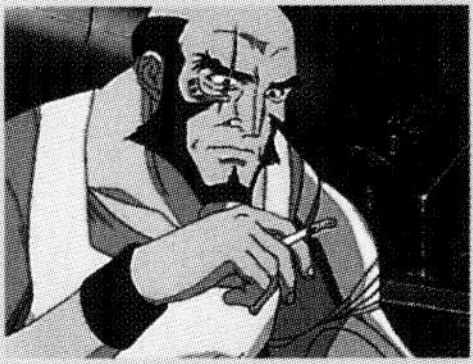

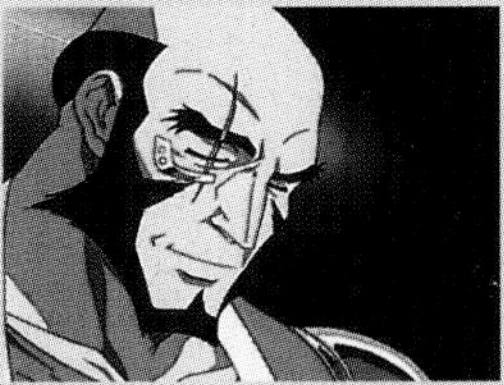

21 Jet says, "That's a good story," but Spike replies, "I hate that story." Spike smiles mischievously and says, "I hate cats." "I thought so…" Jet grins. They both erupt into laughter.

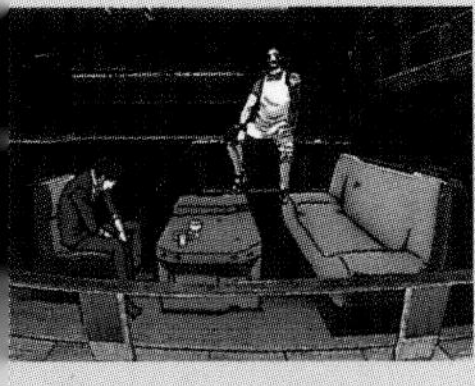

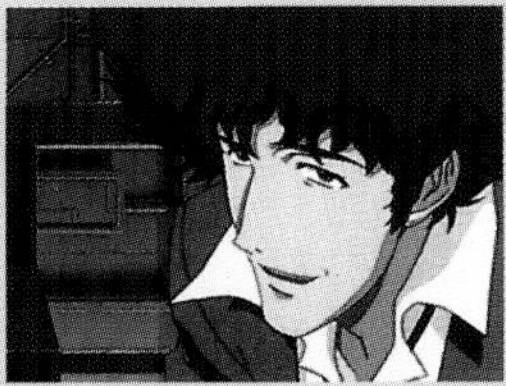

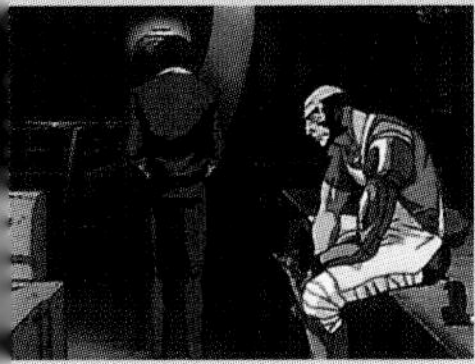

"There's nothing I can do for a woman who is already dead."

22 After a good laugh, Spike gets up to leave. "Can I ask you one thing?" Jet calls out. "Is it for a woman?" Spike looks back a little and says, "There's nothing I can do for a woman who is already dead."

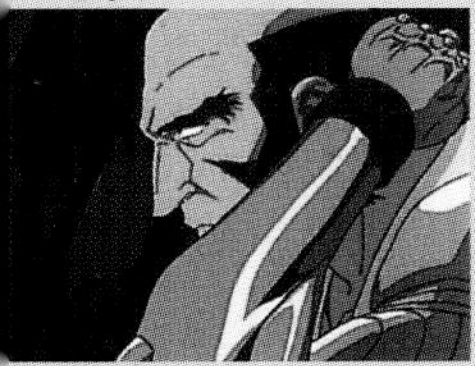

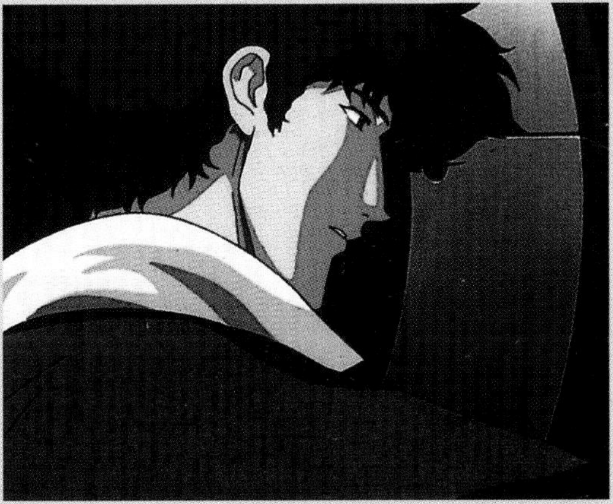

23 As Spike goes to leave, Faye aims a gun at his head. "Where are you going?" When he doesn't answer, she says, "You told me once that the past doesn't matter. YOU'RE the one who is caught up in the past."

"I've always looked with one eye on the past. And with the other eye on the present."

24 Spike moves his face close to Faye and asks her to look at his eyes. "One is fake, because I lost it in an accident. Ever since then, I've always kept one eye on the past... I've always felt that what I see isn't a reality." For the first time, Spike tells Faye about himself.

25 "Don't, talk like that... You never told me anything about yourself before! So don't tell me stuff like that now!" Spike tells her, "I thought I was watching a dream I would never wake up from." Then with a mocking smile on his face, he says, "Before I knew it, the dream was over." He turns to leave.

SESSION#26

26 Faye tells him, "I got my memories back." Spike stops. Faye continues, "But nothing good came of it…There was no place for me to go back to." All of the emotions she's kept bottled up since her cyrogentic sleep come welling to the surface. "This is the only place I have to come back to!"

INTERLUDE

In this session, the words that usually appear at the end of the episode, "SEE YOU SPACE COWBOY…" are replaced with "YOU"RE GONNA CARRY THAT WEIGHT." This is drawn from the lyrics of a song called "CARRY THAT WEIGHT," which was recorded by the Beatles and appears on their 1969 album "Abbey Road." (Continued on pg. 56)

"I'm going to find out if I'm truly alive."

27 "Where are you going?" Faye screams. "Why are you going? Are you just going to throw your life away?" Spike answers, "I'm not going to die. I'm going to find out if I'm truly alive."

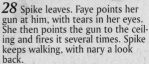

28 Spike leaves. Faye points her gun at him, with tears in her eyes. She then points the gun to the ceiling and fires it several times. Spike keeps walking, with nary a look back.

29 Stricken with grief, Faye can't hold back her tears. Meanwhile, Jet focuses his pain into polishing the windows on the bridge, the expression on his face devoid of all emotion…

30 In the cockpit, Spike is overcome with images of the past, spinning through his mind like a kaleidoscope. His love for Julia, his friendship with Vicious. Vicious sits in the seat of power, awaiting Spike imminent's arrival.

INTERLUDE

As mentioned on page 55, the words from the final scene are from the Beatles song, "Carry That Weight." This song was designed as a message to their fans that they were going to break up. The "Bebop" staff uses the song as a message to its fans that the series is coming to an end. Those who are interested may want to take a look at the lyrics of the song.

SESSION#26

31 Spike rushes the Red Dragon headquarters. Caught off gaurd, the syndicate men attack with intense gunfire, and block Spike's way!

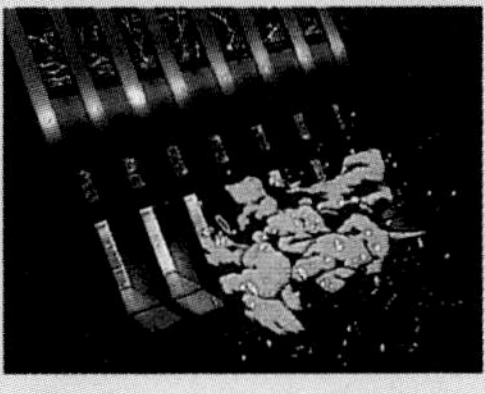

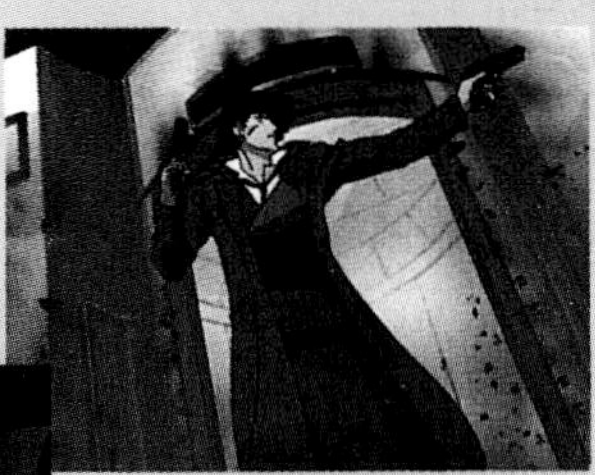

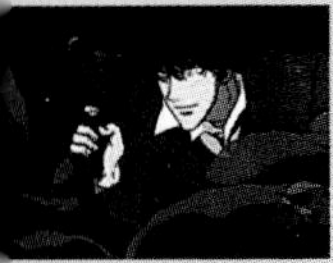

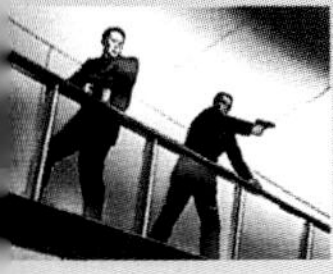

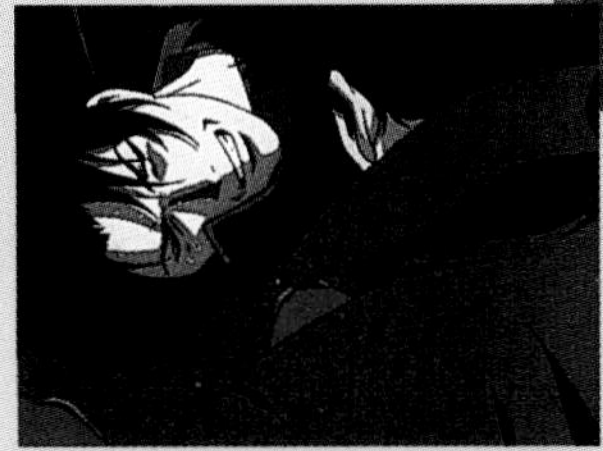

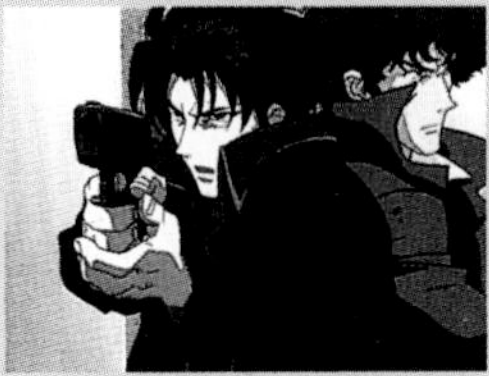

32 Spike rides the elevator but gets hit coming out. Shin appears, though, to back him up. Shin explains that Vicious is on the top floor and proceeds to lead Spike there.

33 On the way to the roof, Shin is felled by an enemy attack. Spike runs up to him. In a broken voice, Shin tells Spike, "Actually…I was hoping you'd come back," and then dies.

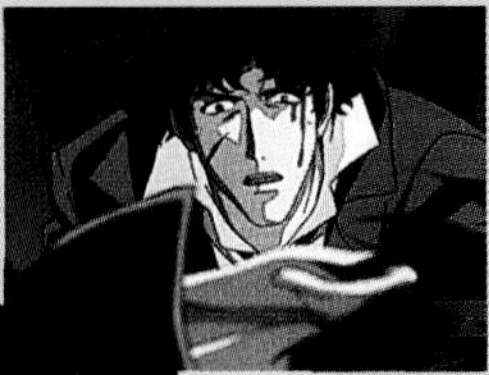

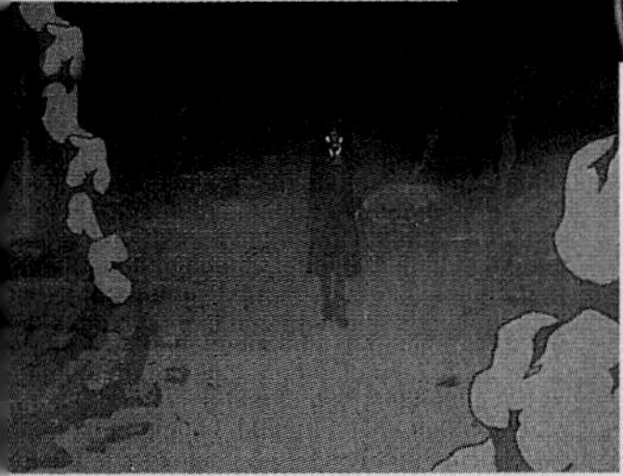

"I am the only one who can kill you."

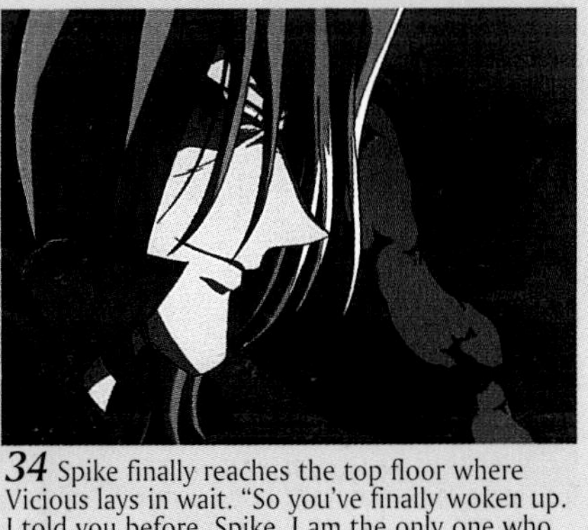

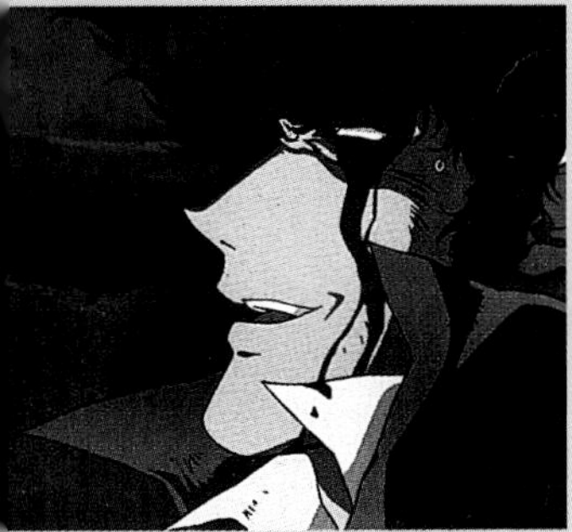

34 Spike finally reaches the top floor where Vicious lays in wait. "So you've finally woken up. I told you before, Spike. I am the only one who can kill you." Spike answers, "I'll send those words back to you, Vicious. Either way, it was our destiny to end up like this."

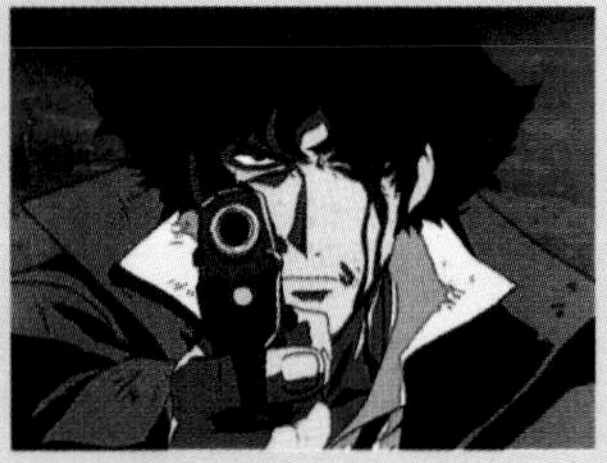

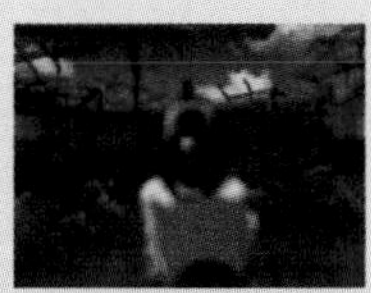

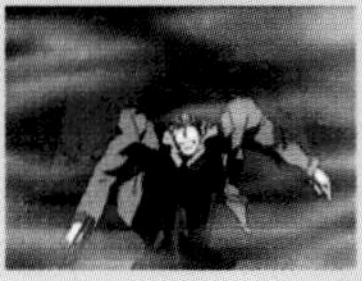

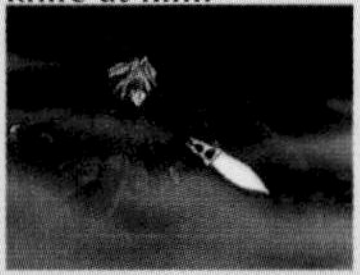

35 Spike aims at Vicious and pulls the trigger. But because of the wound above his left eye, his aim is off and he misses. Spike comes racing up the stairs, and Vicious throws a knife at him.

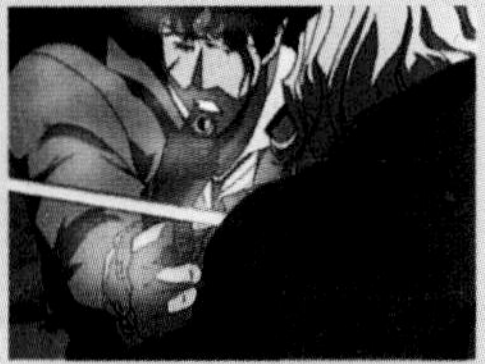

36 Spike fires on Vicious, Vicious slashes at Spike. They both evade each others' attacks. They go face to face, steel against steel. Their opposing forces repel one another, and both of their weapons fly out of their hands!

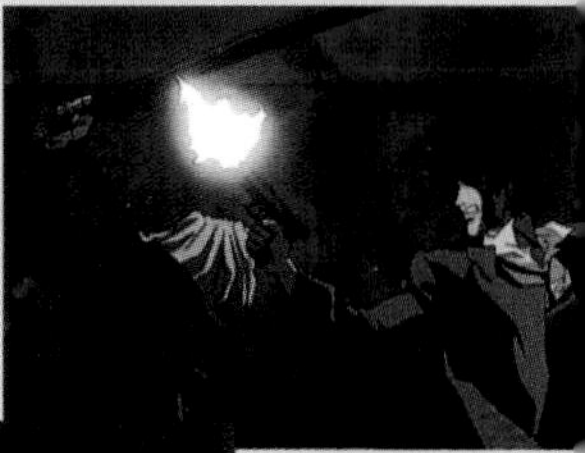

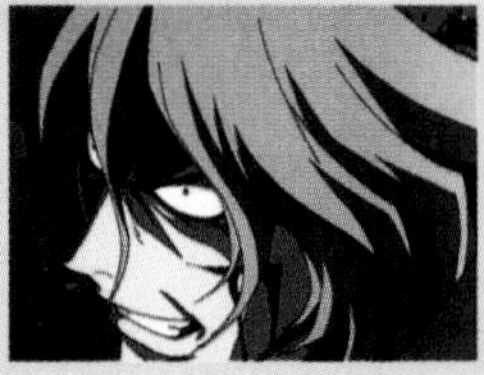

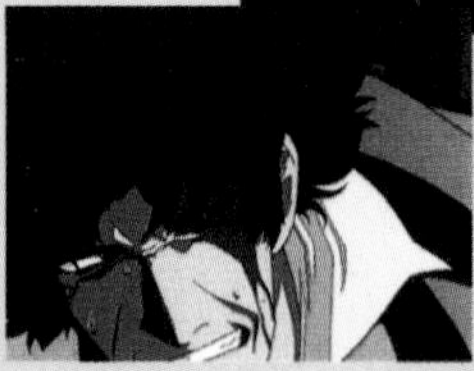

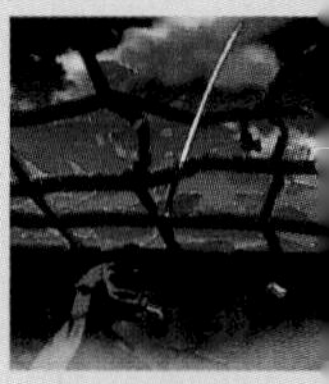

"Let's end this." "As you wish."

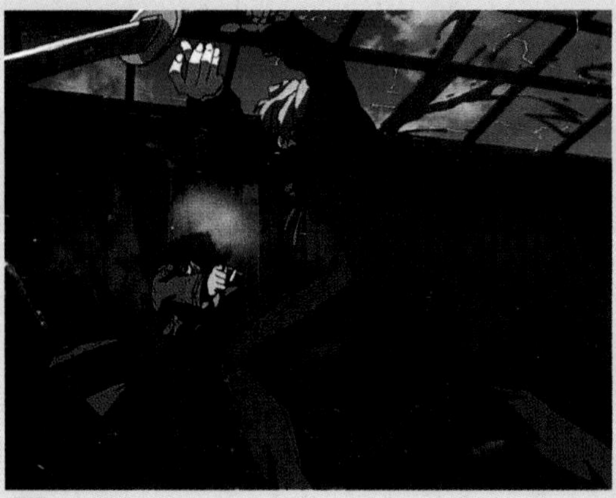

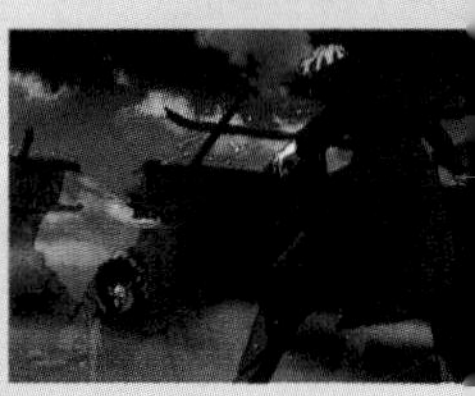

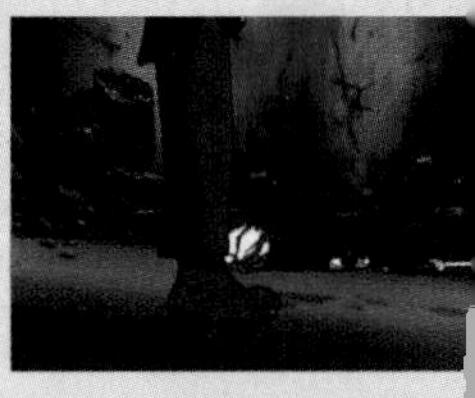

37 The two glare at each other, each one holding down the others' weapon. "Let's end this," Spike says. "As you wish," Vicious answers. They clash again, and Vicious falls.

SESSION#26

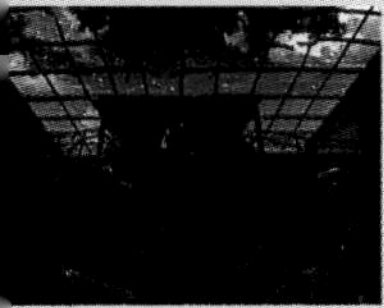
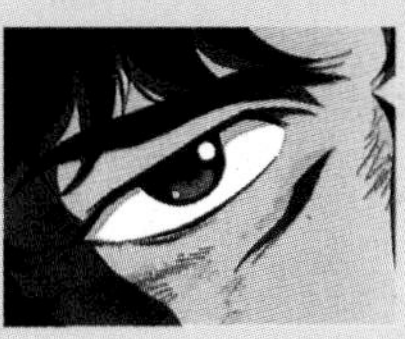

38 Spike has played out his dream. As he gazes up at the sky, he sees an image of Julia just before she died. She asks, "This is a dream, right?" Spike answers, "Yeah, a bad dream." Spike's image is reflected in Julia's eyes.

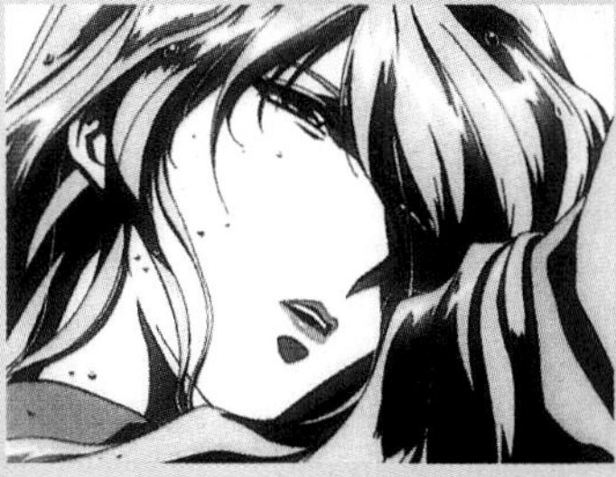

"This is…a dream, right?"
"Yeah…A bad dream."

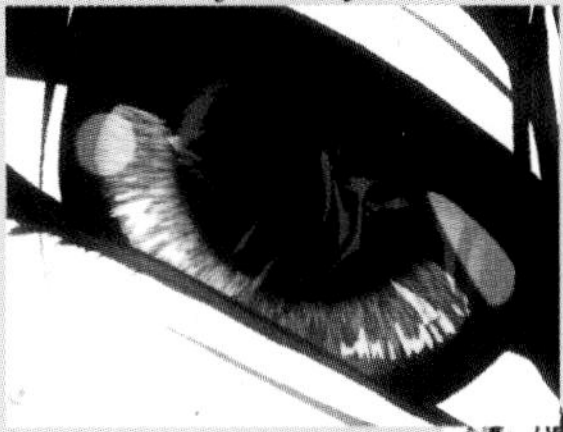

"Bang."

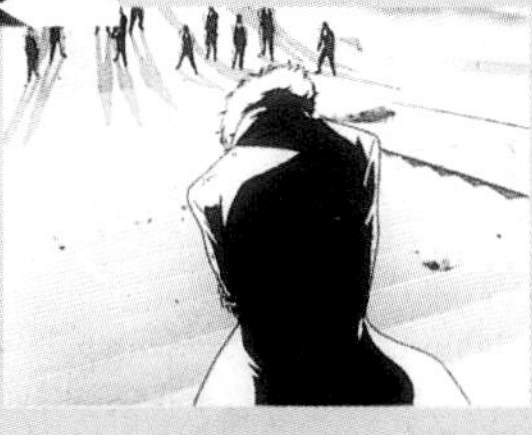
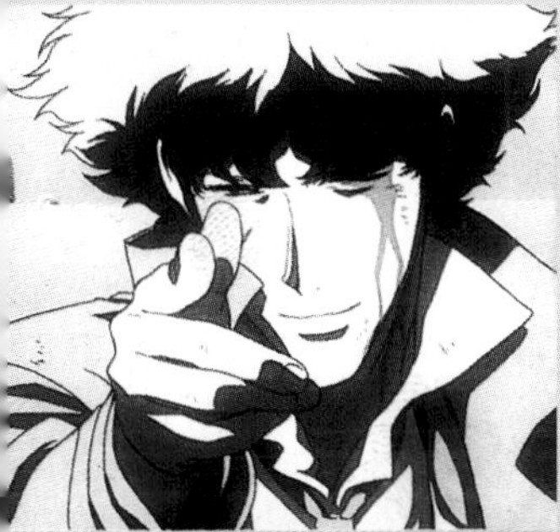
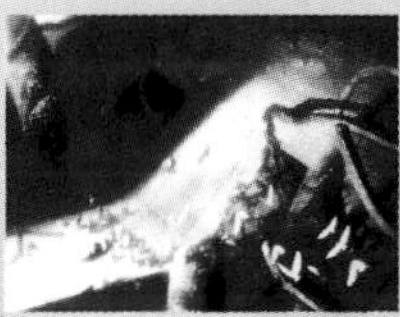
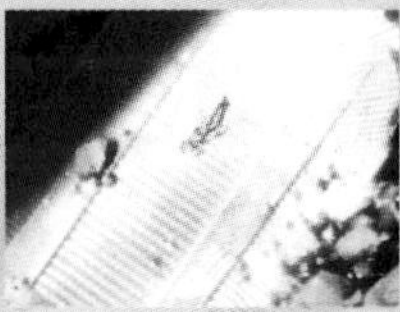
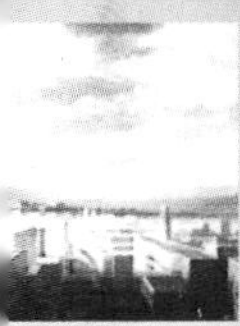
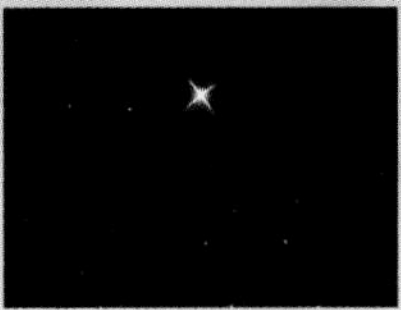

39 The lobby of the Red Dragon headquarters. Seriously wounded, Spike stumbles down the stairs. Smirking, he pretends to aim a gun at the men watching him, and then collapses from his wounds. And just then, the twinkle of a single star in the distant sky above, slowly disappears.

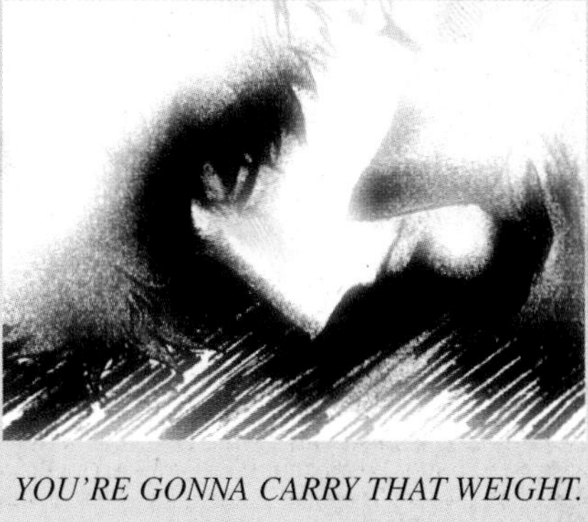

YOU'RE GONNA CARRY THAT WEIGHT.

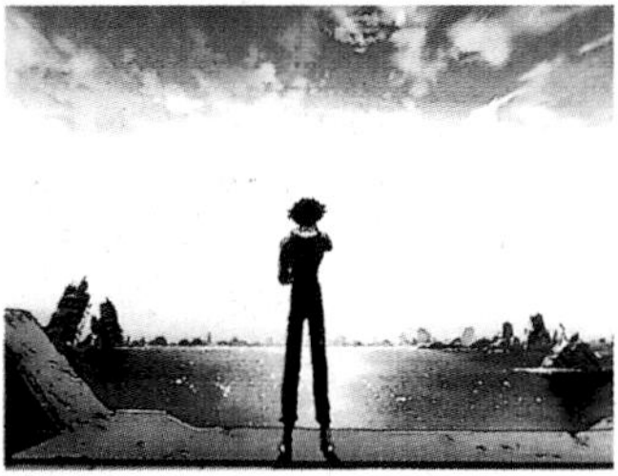

COWBOY REPORT

PART I

Art Board Introduction (3)

These are the numerous artboards that were drawn to accent the effect of the climax, making it even more impressive. The scenery of Session 24 in particular is breathtakingly beautiful.

SESSION #24

「"Hard Luck Women"」

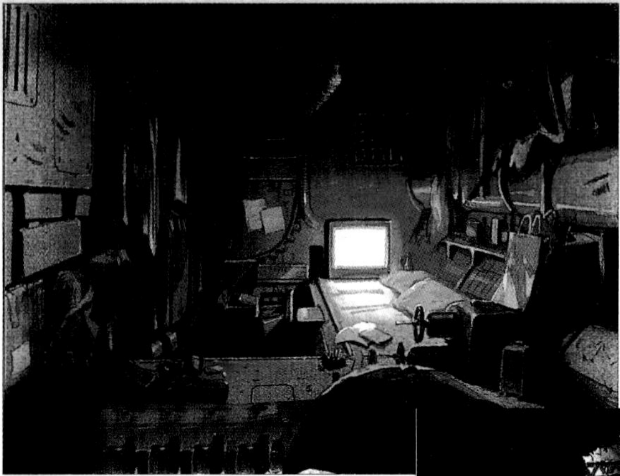

Faye's room
Finally making its appearance close to the end, Faye's quarters on the Bebop is littered with junk haphazardly tossed around the room (she seems to have a lot of clothes). Rather than being 'dirty,' there simply seems to be an endless amount of stuff. As cluttered as her mind, perhaps.

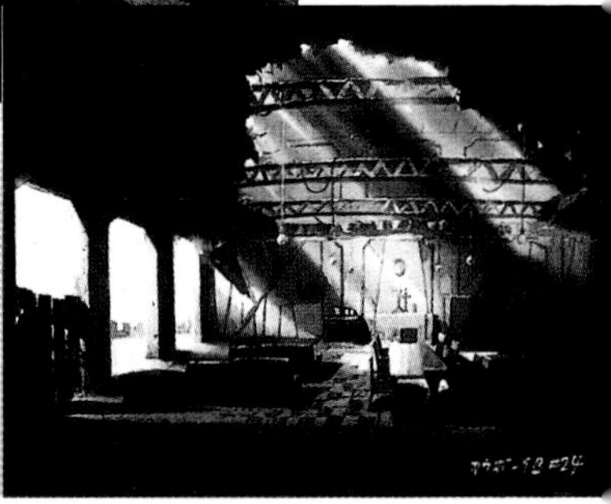

The convent:
Ed and Faye visit here while on Earth. Ed had lived here for a while. Sunlight filters in through the dilapidated ceiling, creating a very peaceful atmosphere. The table in the center is where Ed, Faye, and the orphans have their meal.

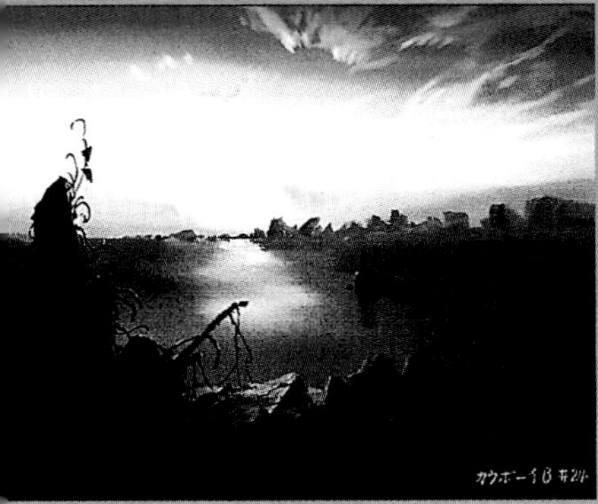

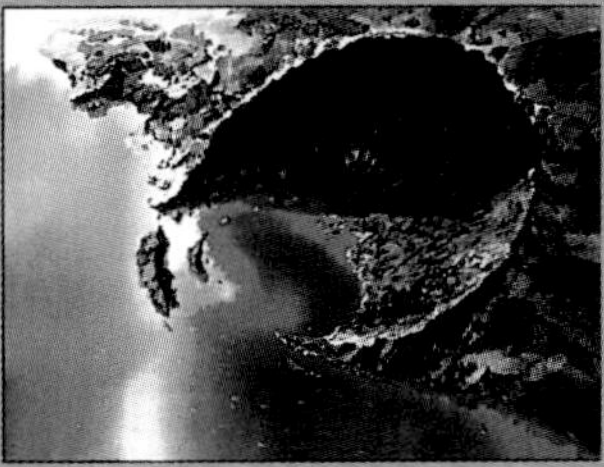

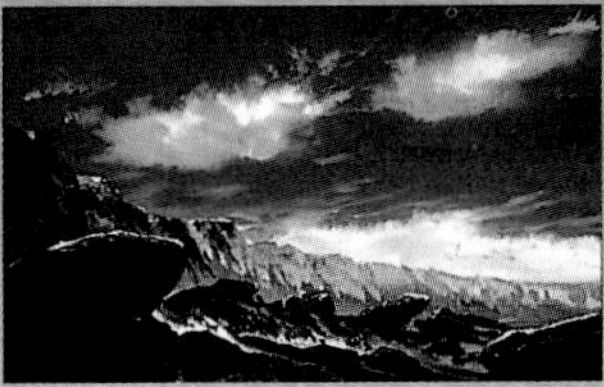

ie battered earth

e earth has been battered by meteorites that fall from the ·on. Most of the cities have been turned into ruins, leaving hind lakes and craters.

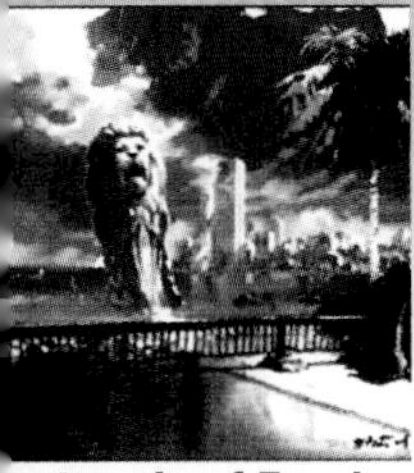

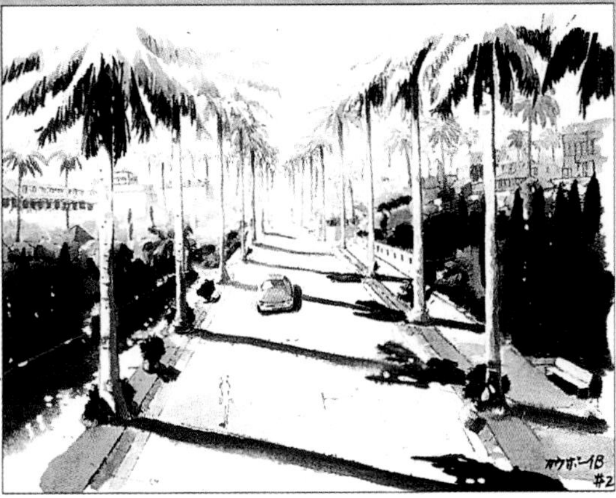

ie terrain of Faye's emories

ese are vague reflections of ye's memory. When she reach- it, a seaside park leaves a nt impression in her mind. ove is that seaside park. To left is the road that Faye nembers leading to her house.

Interview with art director Jun'ichi Higashi (1)

The park that Faye stops at is set in Singapore, and it was modeled after a real park in Singapore. The merlion statue and such are pretty close to the real thing. And also, the color of the sky and sea are modeled after those of southern countries; I paid careful attention to give it a bright color tone.

The fact that Faye's room is messy was decided in the scenario phase. Looking at the rejected setting materials, I adapted them in my own way as I drew. And I remember that the dilapidated convent that came up is essentially exactly according to the setting materials, and the director told me to give it the image of "a different atmosphere, cut off from the outside world."

The scene I paid most attention to in this session is the parting scene in the second half. To make it as impressive as possible, I paid careful attention to the colors of the sunset, and as I drew it, I kept in mind expressing a certain kind of "bittersweetness."

SESSION #25

"The Real Folk Blues (Part 1)"

Street

This is the street, in some city on Mars, down which Julia runs in the beginning of the story. The stone pavement, cloudy sky, and the classic buildings all are evokative of noir cityscapes. The entire session makes a lot of use of muted colors.

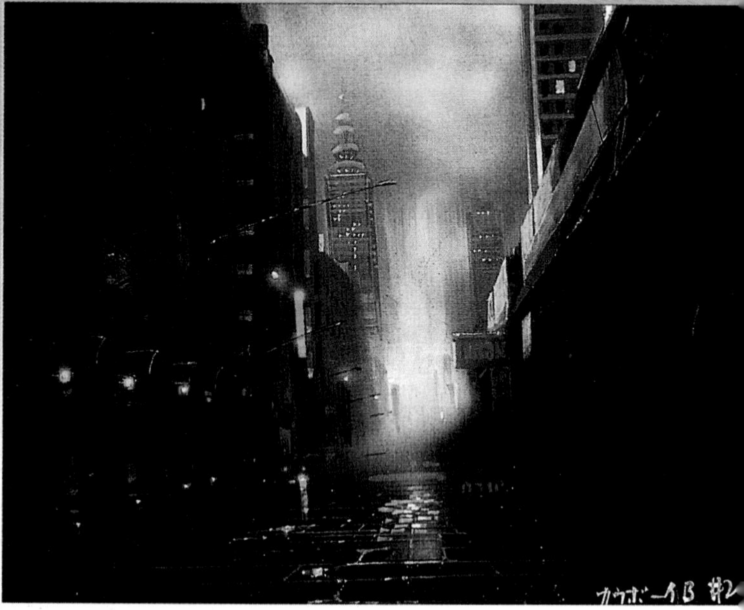

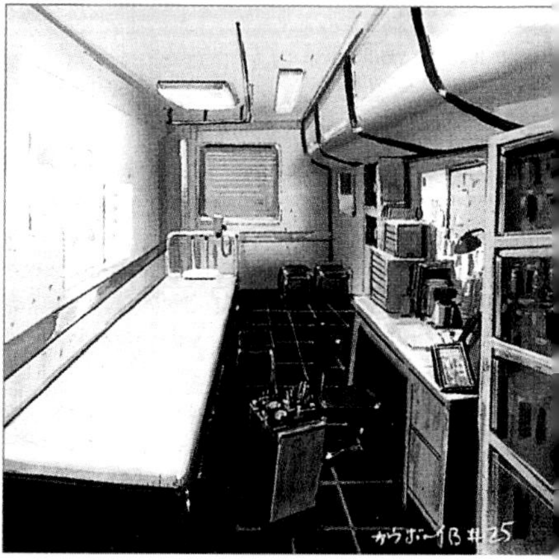

The doctor's office

The office of the "doctor" who also appears in Session 2. As befits a "doctor" who really isn't a doctor, there isn't much modern equipment. Only a particular breed patient comes here.

The Red Dragon elders' room

Vicious and his men sneak into this room when they make their nocturnal attack. The elders sit at the landing at the middle of the stairs, and their subordinates lie in wait on the upper corridors. It makes use of Asian color tones, and of course, stately furniture.

Graveyard

Where Spike and Julia are reunited. Three years before, Spike wanted to run away with Julia, and this was the place they were to meet. The design of the gravestones, gives the locale a western-style .

Interview with art director Jun'ichi Higashi (2)

The setting for Sessions 24 and 25 isn't a very pretty world, but rather depicts the underbelly of society. I emphasized the use of somber colors to produce monotone images.

But I added some contrast. To give the Red Dragon building a Chinese atmosphere with a stateliness fitting the Chinese mafia, I was particular wanted to use things like Chinese vermilion, and ornate furniture.

For the last scene, when Spike finaly collapses, I used the imagery of a world covered almost completely in white, and tried to create the impression that this may or may not be reality. This is what the director requested.

SESSION #26

"The Real Folk Blues (Part 2)"

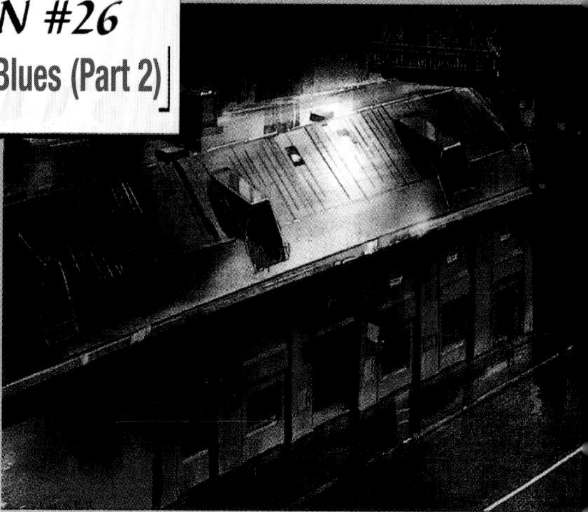

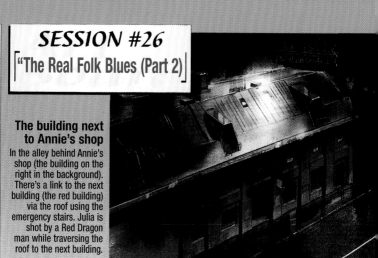

The building next to Annie's shop

In the alley behind Annie's shop (the building on the right in the background). There's a link to the next building (the red building) via the roof using the emergency stairs. Julia is shot by a Red Dragon man while traversing the roof to the next building.

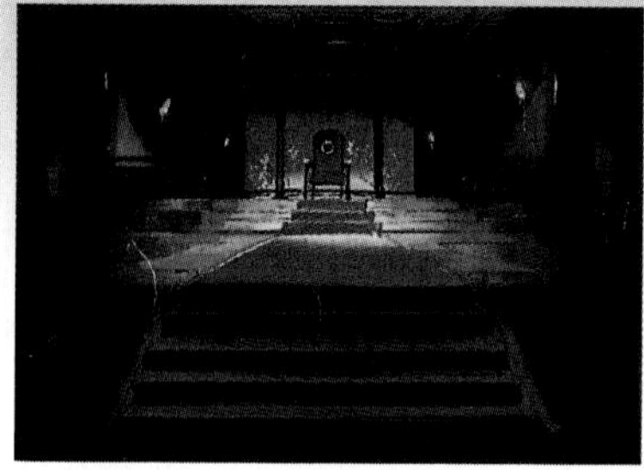

Red Dragon building, ceremony roo

The top floor of the Red Dragon building. In the second half of the story, Vicious awaits Spike's arrival seated in the chair in the center. During Spi and Vicious' final battle, the roof is blown away by an explosion.

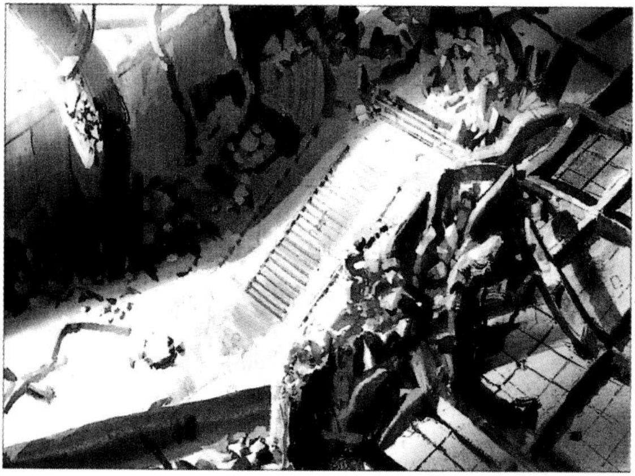

The ruined Red Dragon building

From the final scene, when Spike loses his strength and collapses. From this angle, the camera pans up to the sky, leading into the ending theme. Among all the numerous final chapters that use gloomy scenery, this is a uniquely bright artboard.

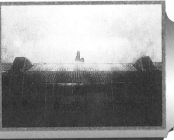

COWBOY REPORT
PART II

Complete Song List (Part 3)

Introducing the BGM used in Sessions 24~26. Note the various songs that color these episodes, the climax of the series.

Session #24 "Hard Luck Women"

Session #24
ハード・ラック・ウーマン

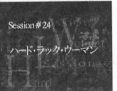

The scene where Appledelhi appears
"ADIEU" ***

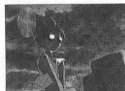

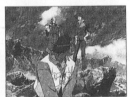

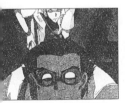

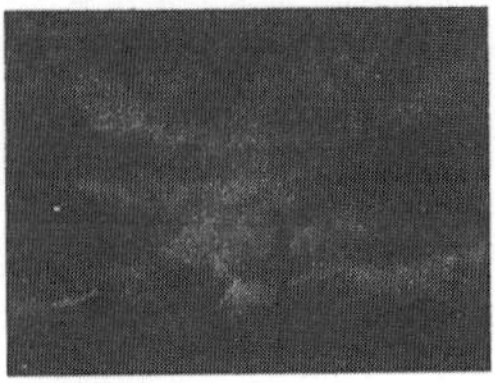

The conversation at the orphanage
"OMAKE FINAL MIX (New Song)"

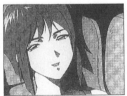

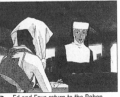

3 Ed and Faye return to the Bebop
"WALTZ for ZIZI" *

4 Faye's flashback scene
"WO QUI NON COIN" ***

5 "Poor Faye (a feeling of hope)"

The highlight of this session is the song that plays during Ed's exit scene, titled "Call Me, Call Me." There are no words spoken during this sequence, but the melody and lyrics of this song seem to speak the character's feelings instead. "Omake Final Mix," which isn't on any soundtrack, has a baseline that bears close resemblance to the one in the Beetles song "Come Together."

6 Spike and Jet come to nab Appledelhi
"Don't Bother none" **

7 Ed's departure
"CALL ME CALL ME" ***

* Included on "OST 1"
** Included on "OST 2 – No Disc –"
*** Included on "OST 3 – Blue –"
V Included on "Vitaminless"
If a song does not have one of those symbols next to its title, it is not yet included on a soundtrack.
(All of these are provisional titles)

Session #25 "The Real Folk Blues (Part 1)"

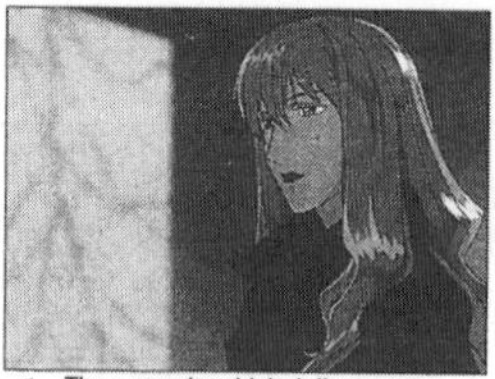

1 The scene in which Julia appears
"ADIEU" ***

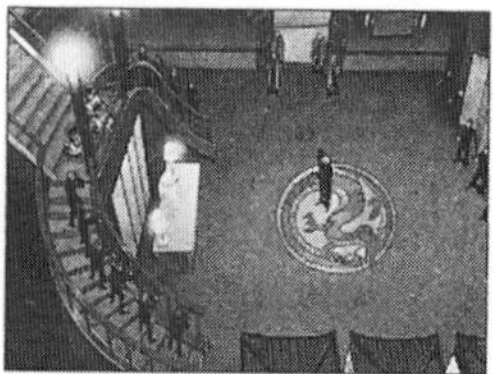

2 The conversation between Vicious and the elders
"Space Noh"

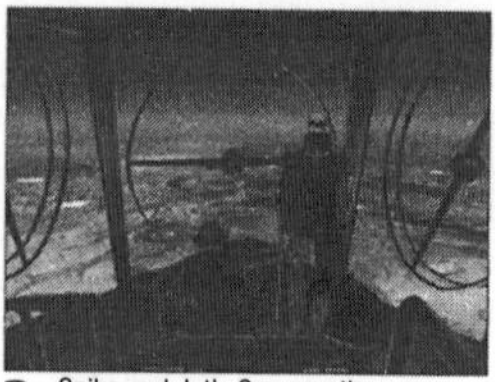

3 Spike and Jet's Conversation
"WALTZ for ZIZI" *

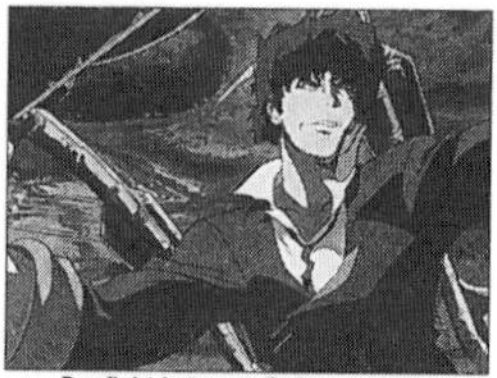

4 Dogfight between Spike and the Red Dragon Syndicate
"ROAD TO THE WEST" ***

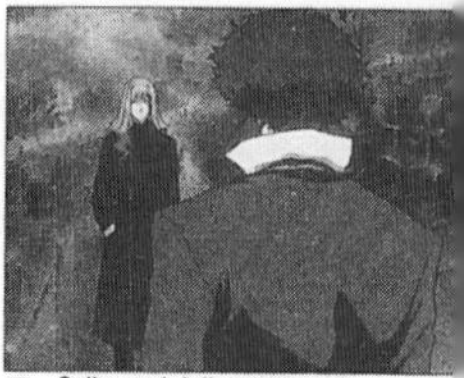

5 Spike and Julia meet again
"MEMORY" *

This session, the first of a two-part story, uses very little music, and what is used is minimalist in nature. The most striking song is "Road to the West," which plays during the dogfight between Spike and the Red Dragon men chasing after him. The action builds to the languid melody of the saxophone in scenes such as Vicious' entrance, and the Bebop in battle.

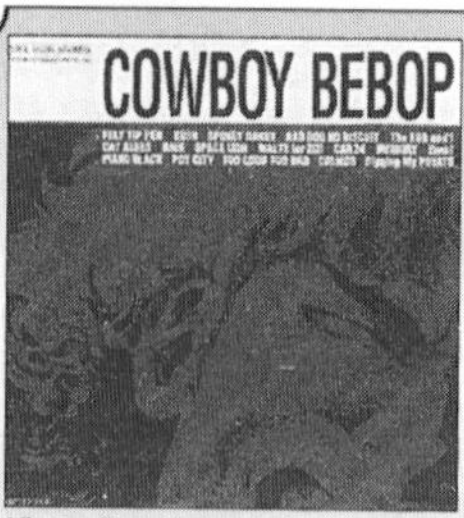
COWBOY BEBOP

Victor Entertainment
VICL-60201

1st ORIGINAL SOUNDTRACK

COWBOY BEBOP

1. Tank! 2. RUSH 3. SPOKEY DOKEY 4. BAD DOG NO BISCUITS 5. CAT BLUES 6. COSMOS 7. SPACE LION 8. WALTZ FOR ZIZI 9. PIANO BLACK 10. POT CITY 11. TOO GOOD TOO BAD 12. CAR 24 13. The EGG and I 14. FELT TIP PEN 15. RAIN 16. DIGGING MY POTATO 17. MEMORY

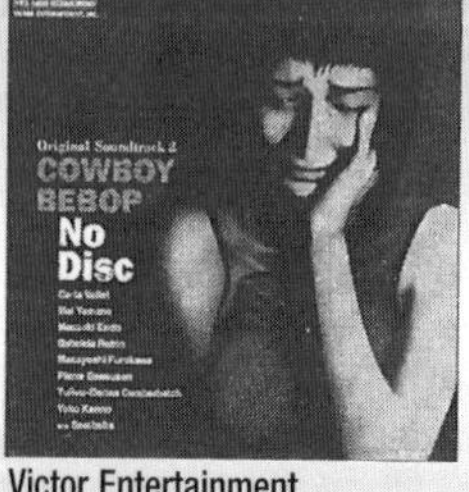
Original Soundtrack 2
COWBOY
BEBOP
No
Disc

Victor Entertainment
VICL-60202

2nd ORIGINAL SOUNDTRACK

COWBOY BEBOP No Disc

1. American Money 2. Fantaisie Sign 3. Don't Bother None 4. Vitamin A 5. LIVE in Baghdad 6. Cats on Mars 7. Want It All Back 8. Bindy 9. You make me cool 10. Vitamin B 11. Green Bird 12. ELM 13. Vitamin C 14. Gateway 15. The Singing Sea 16. The EGG and YOU 17. Forever Broke 18. POWER OF KUNG FOOD REMIX

Session #26 "The Real Folk Blues (Part 2)"

1 Julia talks of the past
"MEMORY" *

2 Spike leaves the Bebop
"Forever Broke" **

3 Spike attacks the Red Dragon building
"SEE YOU SPACE COWBOYS NOT FINAL MIX MOUNTAIN ROOT" ***

This session is distinguished from the others in that it uses few songs, but the songs it does use are played for a long length of time. Among them is "See You Space Cowboys," a different arrangement of the ending theme, "The Real Folk Blues." Also, "Blue," which was written for the last scene, is beautifully played to its full length (about 5 minutes!)

5 Ending
"BLUE" ***

COWBOY BEBOP BLUE

Victor Entertainment
VICL-60203 (Initial pressing comes with a translucent blue jacket)

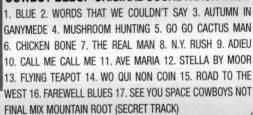

3rd ORIGINAL SOUNDTRACK

COWBOY BEBOP ORIGINAL SOUNDTRACK-BLUE

1. BLUE 2. WORDS THAT WE COULDN'T SAY 3. AUTUMN IN GANYMEDE 4. MUSHROOM HUNTING 5. GO GO CACTUS MAN 6. CHICKEN BONE 7. THE REAL MAN 8. N.Y. RUSH 9. ADIEU 10. CALL ME CALL ME 11. AVE MARIA 12. STELLA BY MOOR 13. FLYING TEAPOT 14. WO QUI NON COIN 15. ROAD TO THE WEST 16. FAREWELL BLUES 17. SEE YOU SPACE COWBOYS NOT FINAL MIX MOUNTAIN ROOT (SECRET TRACK)

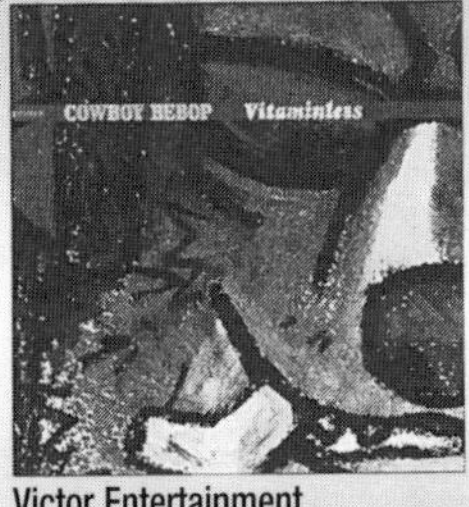

COWBOY BEBOP Vitaminless

Victor Entertainment
VICL-60248

MINI ALBUM

WITAMINLESS

1. THE REAL FOLK BLUES 2. Odd Ones 3. Doggy Dog 4. Cats on Mars 5. SPY 6. Fantaisie Sign 7. Piano Bar I 8. Black Coffee (SECRET TRACK)

CHARACTER FILE

Introducing all of the characters that appear in Session 24~26, along with their names and lines. Right up until the end, quirky characters populate the Bebop world!

Session #2

Appledelhi

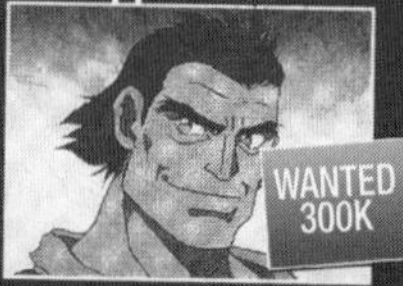
WANTED
300K

"I don't worry about the little things."

Powerful, dynamic, and a slow learner! And on top of that, Ed's father!

MacIntire

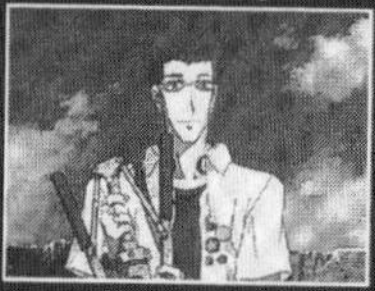

"It's MacIntire!"

He faithfully repeats this same line every single time Appledelhi gets his name wrong,

Clara

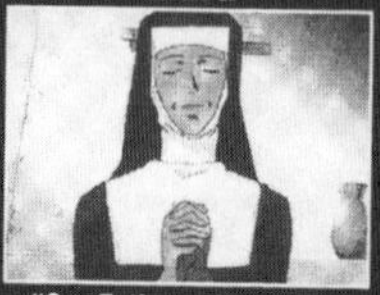

"Our Father, who art in Heaven…you know the rest."

Session #2

Children

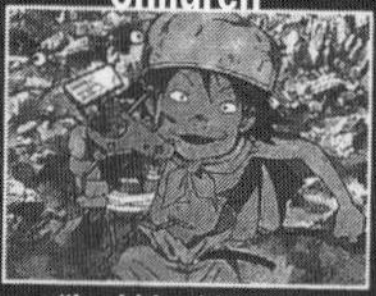

"Look! Look! Look!

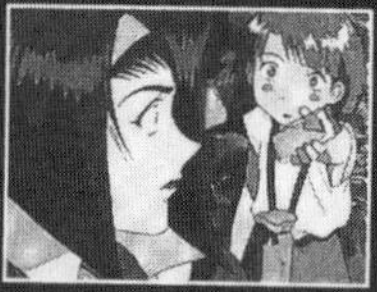

"'Scuse me, can I have your fingernails?"

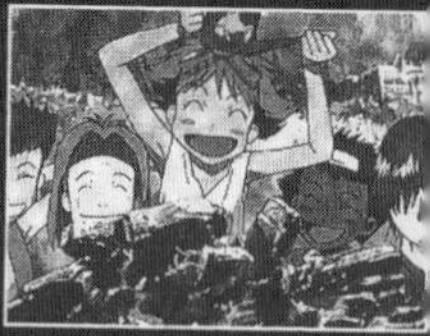

The left-hand picture is Cain, the middle picture is Zuzu. The children in the right-hand picture only appear in one scene, so their names are unknown. They are all orphans who live at Clara's convent. Zuzu likes collecting fingernails, and Cain seems to pride himself on his strange machines.

Session #24

Sally

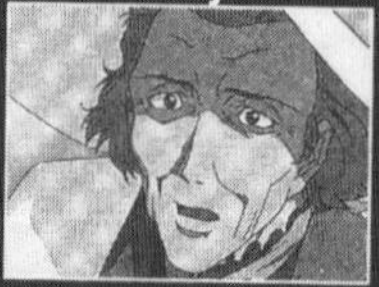

"Are you…Faye?"

One of Faye's classmates in High School, but now an old woman.

Sally's granddaughter

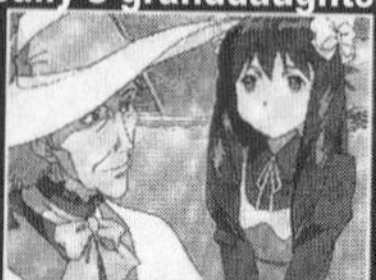

"Grandma, we have to go back now."

A little girl who comes out to see her grandmother. She seems to be a kind-natured girl.

Session #25

Shin

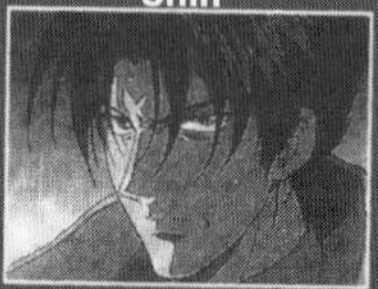

"I was hoping you'd come back."

The younger brother of Lin, who appears in Sessions 12 & 13. A good-looking man who looks like his brother.

Session #25

Wang Long, Suo Long, Pin Long

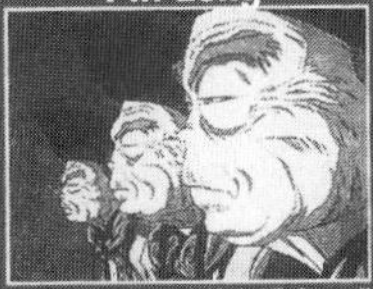

"You look so pitiful, Vicious."

The heads of the Red Dragons. They are wary of Vicious with his radical tendencies.

Bird

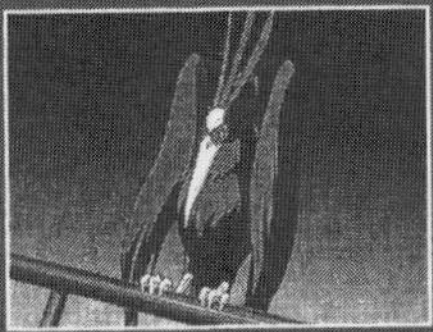

Vicious' pet. Protected its owner by sacrificing its own life.

Doctor

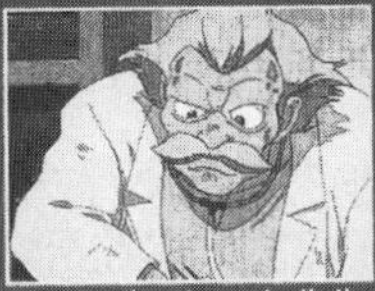

"I'm just treating stray cats, that's all."

He re-appears after Session 2. Has a confidential relationship with Spike and the others.

Session #25

Bob

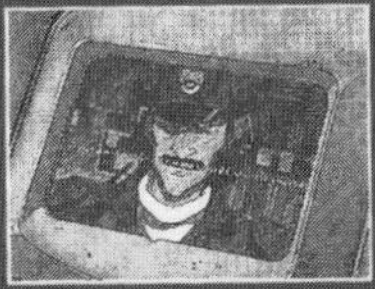

"Get out of there. Even the police can't handle them."

Reappears after Sessions 4 and 20. Jet's main ISSP informant.

Alfred

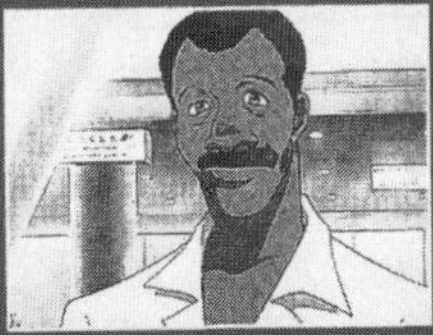

"Punch" was a stage name! He's the ex-host of "Big Shot."

Alfred's mother

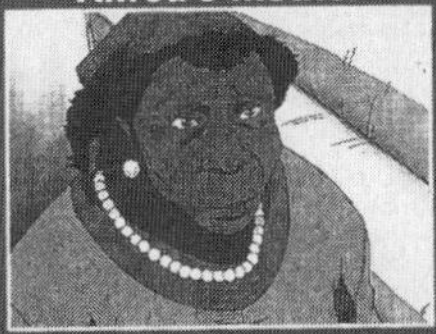

"I ain't talkin'!"

When her little boy asked to live with her, she acted strong at first, but then cried.

Session #25

The elders' subordinates

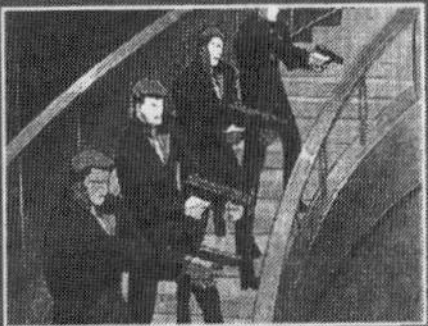

The subordinates of the Red Dragon elders. They face off against Vicious when he makes his moonlight raid.

Red Dragon pursuers (1)

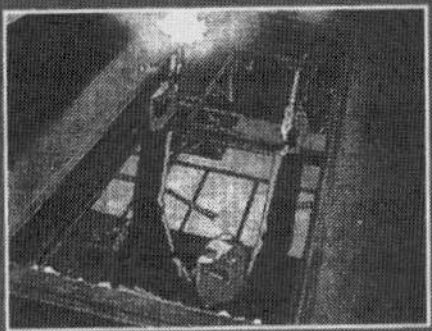

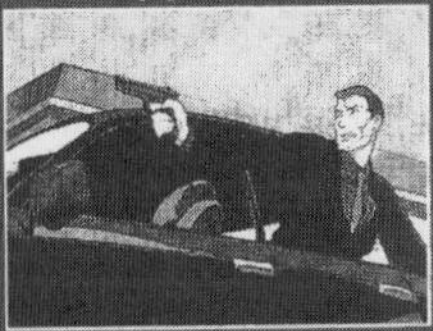

On the left are the men who attacked Spike and Jet as they sit at the bar. On the right are the men who chase after Julia and Faye in their car.

The Story Behind the Story

It's not explicitly stated in the story, but Faye grew up in Singapore. Faye's house (the ruins), which appears in Session 24, is also in Singapore. The official languages of Singapore are Chinese and English, and this is the same as in the era that "Bebop" takes place. This is why there isn't much of a disparity in the way Faye and the others speak, even though she was in cold sleep for 50 years.

And as for "CALL ME SALL ME," the song that plays at the end, when Yoko Kanno played this for the director, Watanabe, he immediately decided to use it for this last scene.

"Without this song, I would have had to make Spike and the others speak. As a matter of fact, in the original scenario, Spike and Jet had dialogue, but I added this song and took out lines." (Director Watanabe)

Session #2

Vicious' subordinate

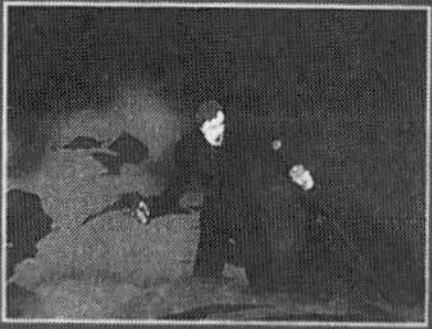

A spy who poses as one of the elders' men, and saves Vicious when he's in trouble.

Red Dragon men (1)

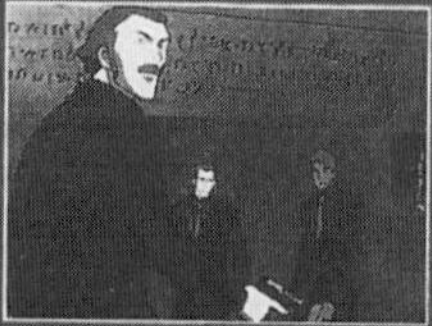

Because the elders are killed by Vicious, these men fall under his command.

Bartender

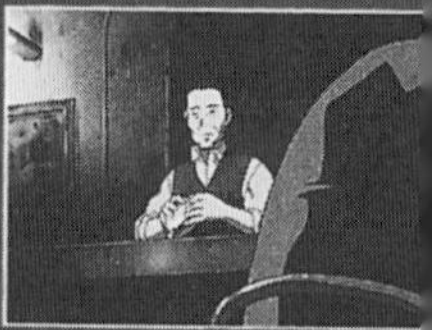

Dies in the crossfire of a shootout. Spike complains about his martini.

Session #2

Annie

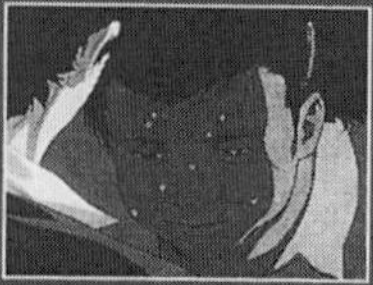

"It's awfully cold today, isn't it?"
Also appears in Session 5. Bound to Spike by a deep trust.

Laughing Bull

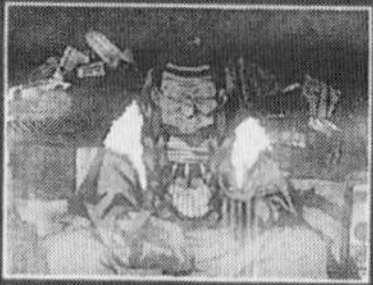

"Do not fear death. Death is always with you."
Appears in Session 1, 12, and 13, and imparts meaningful prophesies.

Red Dragon pursuer (2)

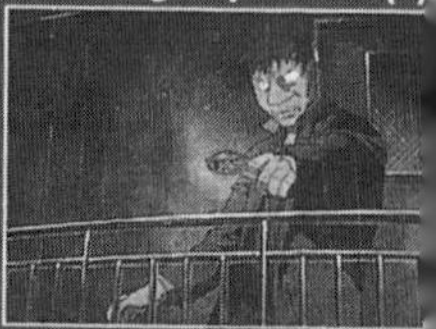

"I ain't talkin'!"
Attacks Spike and Julia. One shot from this man kills Julia.

Session #26

Red Dragon Men (2)

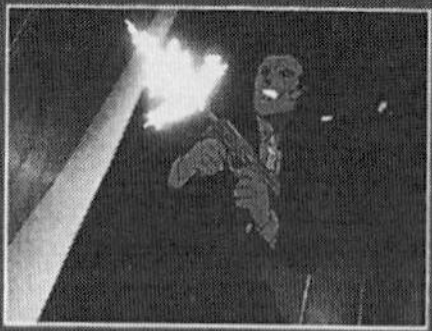

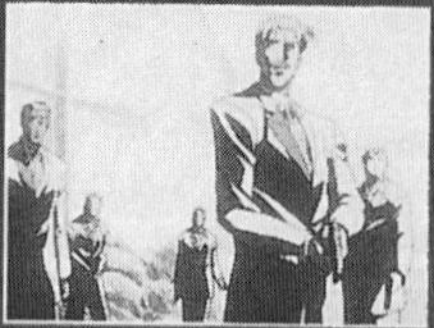

The men in the Red Dragon building. They get into a fierce gunfight with Spike. Shin is shot and killed by the man on the left.

The Story Behind the Story

In magazine interviews and such, the director, Watanabe, usually says that, "The last scene in Session 26 was decided even before Session 1 was finished."

"There seem to be people who think so when they see Spike pale white in the last scene, but…that's wrong. (laugh) Spike goes down the stairs, and then the camera follows flying birds up into the blue sky – and it's not until then that it is complete. In my mind, every last cut determines the flow of the sequence and the composition." (Director Watanabe)

Regarding the song that plays during this scene, "Blue": usually, if Yoko Kanno is doing the recording, the vocals are re-recorded over and over, making them a little more complete each time, but this song was locked with only a single take. The singer Mai Yamane put that much of her soul into it.

Cowboy Bebop
Session #24 ~ #26
Art File *(Guest Characters Part)*

Finally, the climax! Since Sessions 24~26 wrap up the story so far, not many new guests make an appearance. One exception is Appledelhi from Session 24, who leaves quite an impact on the Bebop

SESSION#24

Appledelhi: His full name is Appledelhi Sinis Hesap Lutfen. In order to bring some order back to the battered earth, he observes and makes new maps as the falling meteorites wreak new changes on the earth's topography minute by minute. Ed's father. He's a strong man with a dynamic personality who doesn't bother with details.

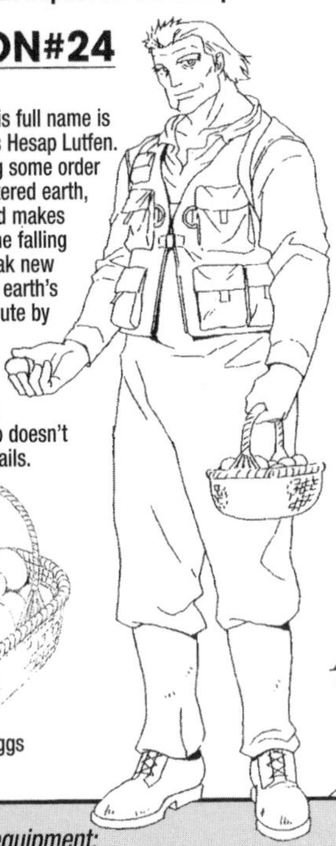

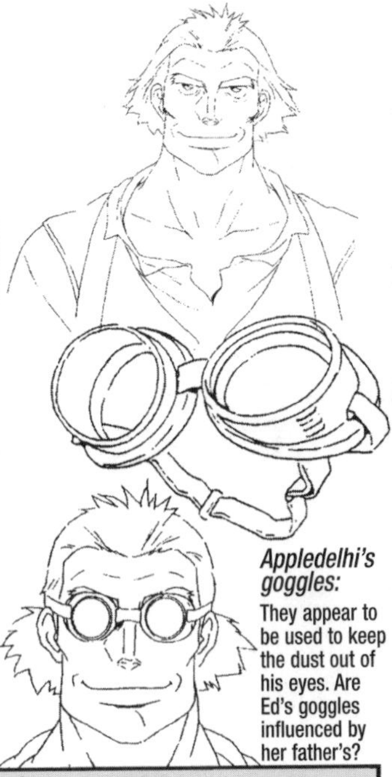

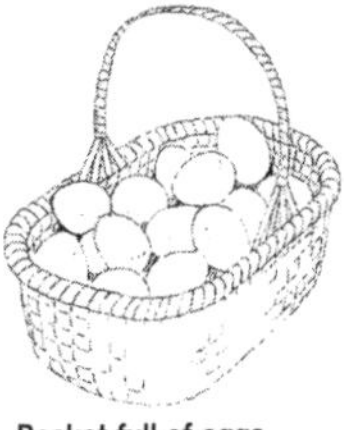

Basket full of eggs

Appledelhi's goggles:
They appear to be used to keep the dust out of his eyes. Are Ed's goggles influenced by her father's?

Deep probe equipment:
Equipment for creating maps. Map data is updated by determining the coordinate position with the anchor, and transmitting it to an artificial satellite with the radar.

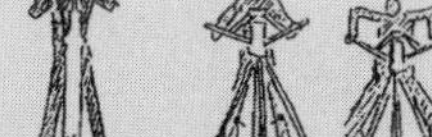

Putting the anchor in the ground

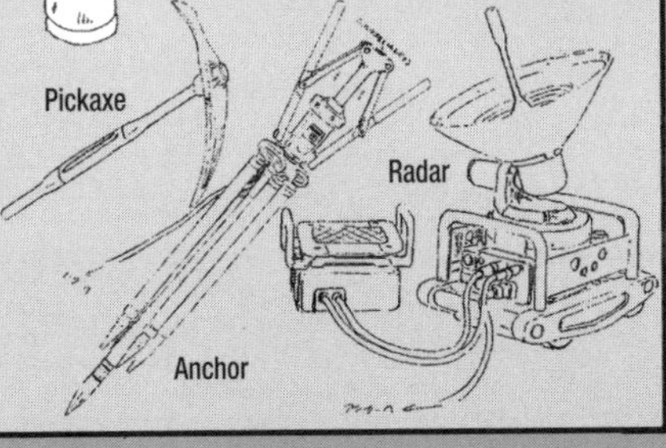
Pickaxe
Radar
Anchor

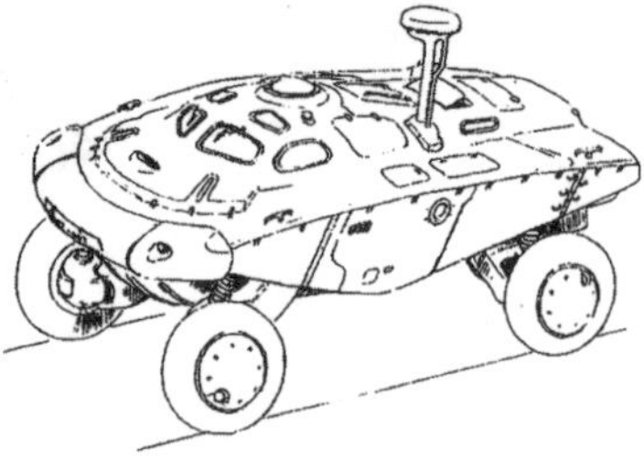

Appledelhi and MacIntire's 4WS car. Equipped with variable compression balloon tires, which are suited for traveling over the rough terrain. For some reason, it's equipped with a bird's nest.

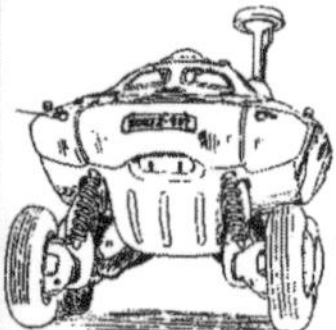

Rear view

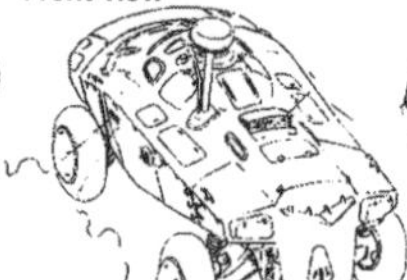

Front view

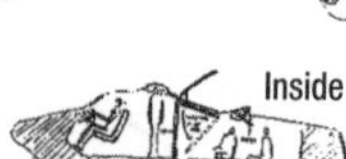

Inside diagram

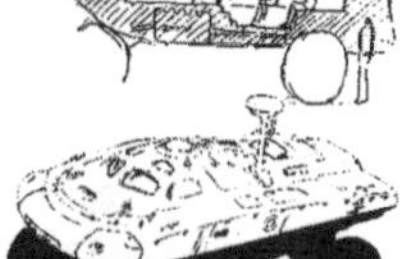

Water-travel: When it cruises on the water, The lower half sinks underwater. It moves by using water jets.

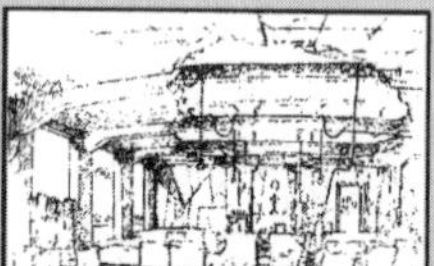

Inside the convent: The interior is rather dilapidated.

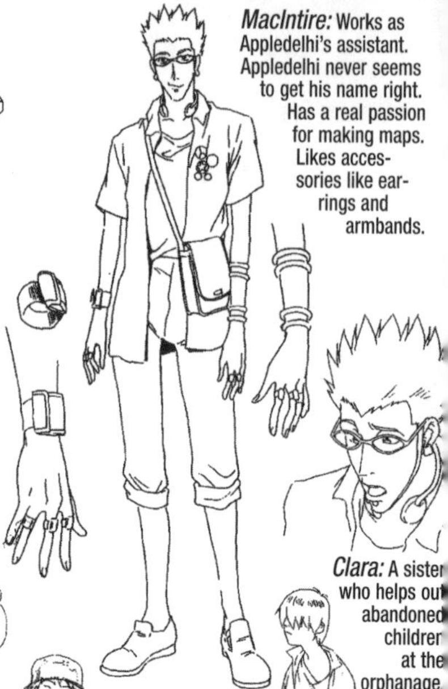

MacIntire: Works as Appledelhi's assistant. Appledelhi never seems to get his name right. Has a real passion for making maps. Likes accessories like earrings and armbands.

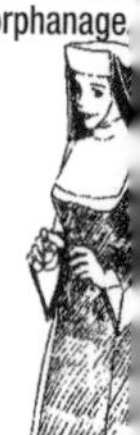

Clara: A sister who helps out abandoned children at the orphanage.

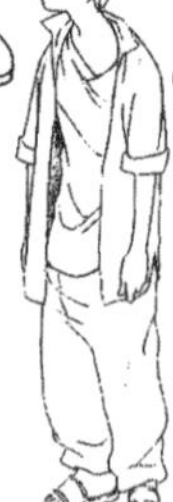

Shawne: A young boy who lives at the orphanage. The baggy clothes and long hair are part of his character.

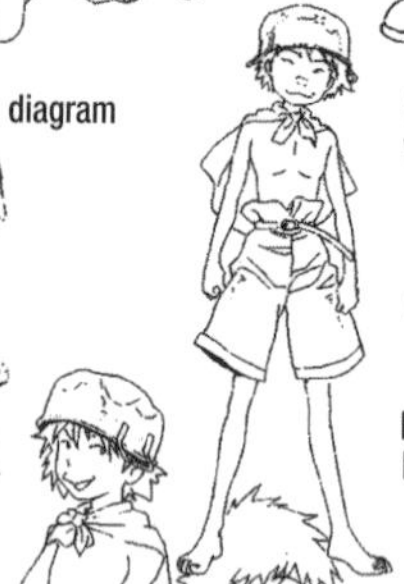

Cain: He wears a handkerchief mantle over an otherwise bare upper body, and a pot for a helmet on his head. He is barefoot too.

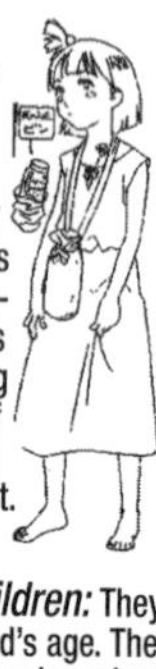

Zuzu: Her hobby is collecting fingernails. She walks around carrying a bottle full of them. Always barefoot.

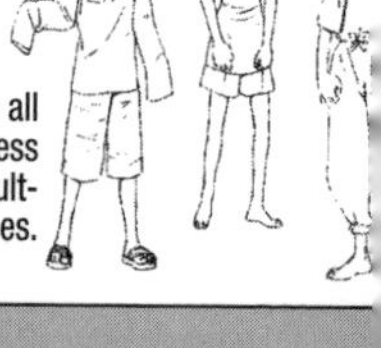

Other Children: They are all around Ed's age. They dress themselves in various adult-size clothes.

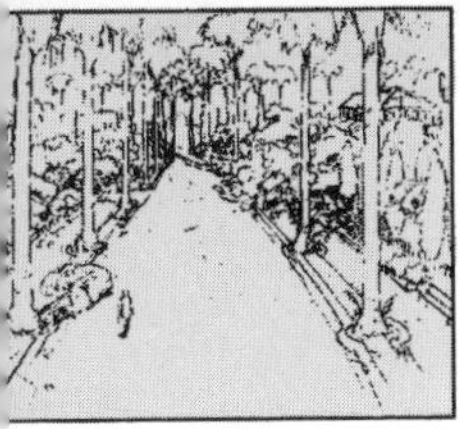

Sally Young: A high school classmate of Faye's. She uses a wheelchair.

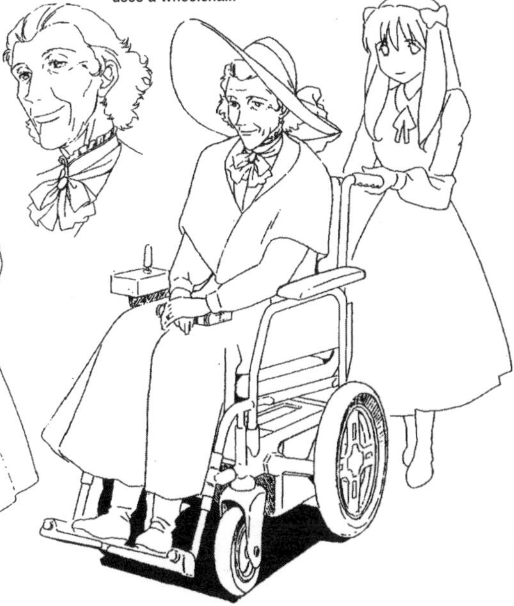

Sally's Granddaughter: The little girl who comes out to see her grandmother.

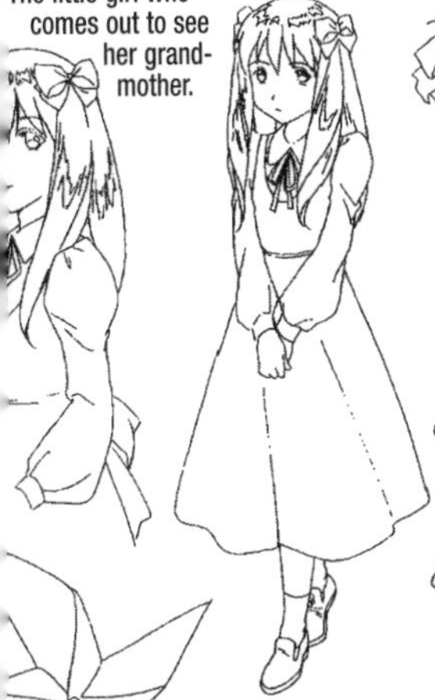

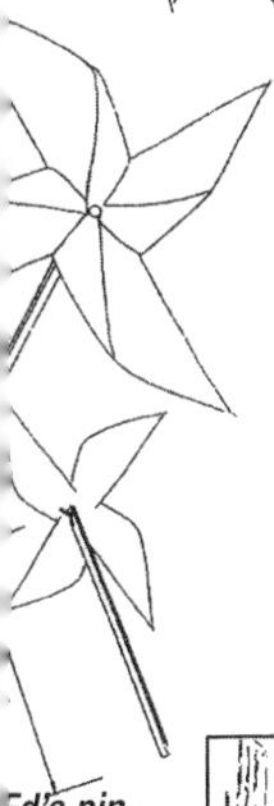

Ed's pin-wheel: Ed ands this o Spike when he leaves the ebop. Ed rought it back vith her from he convent.

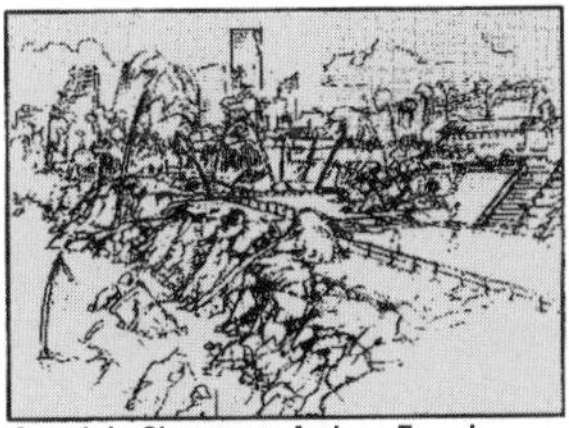

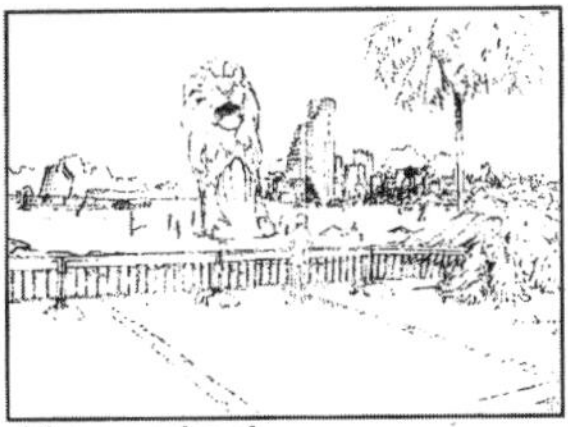

A park in Singapore: A place Faye has some faint memories of.

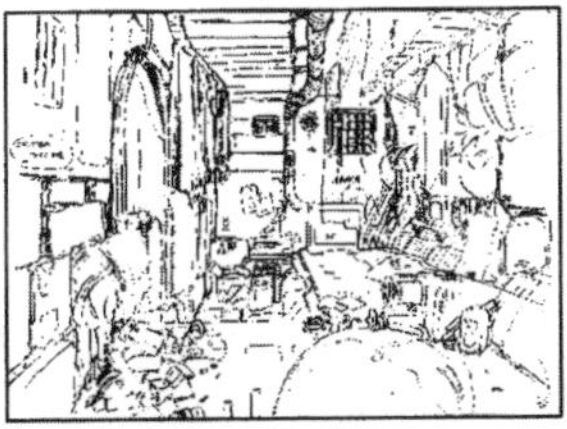

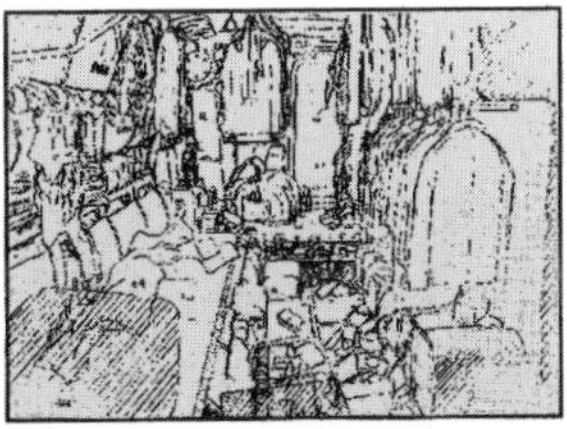

Inside the Bebop – Faye's room

SESSION#25

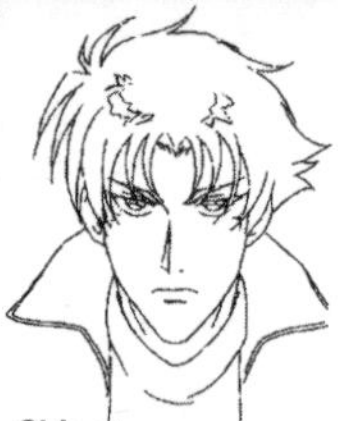

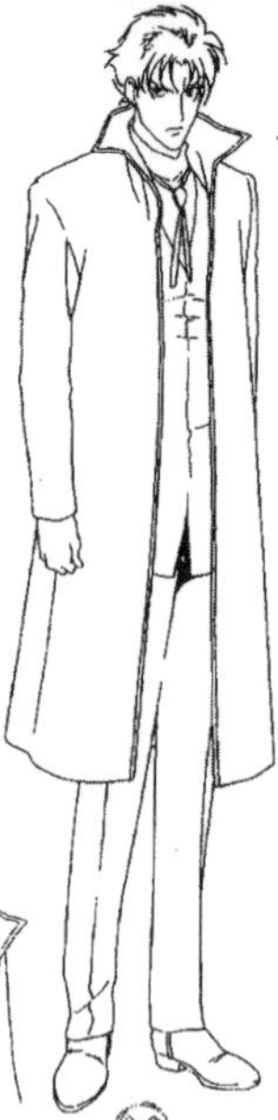

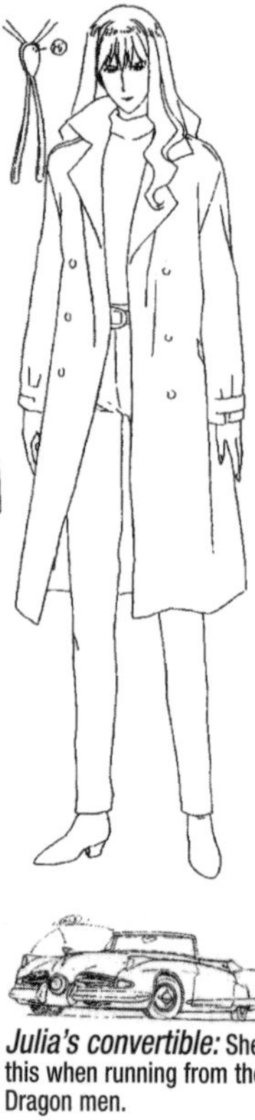

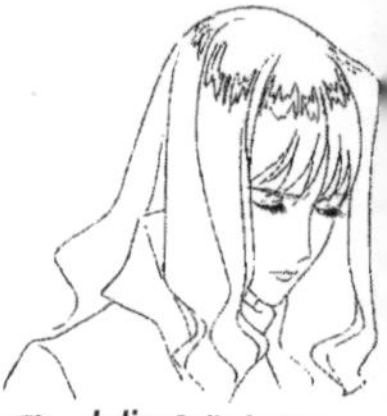

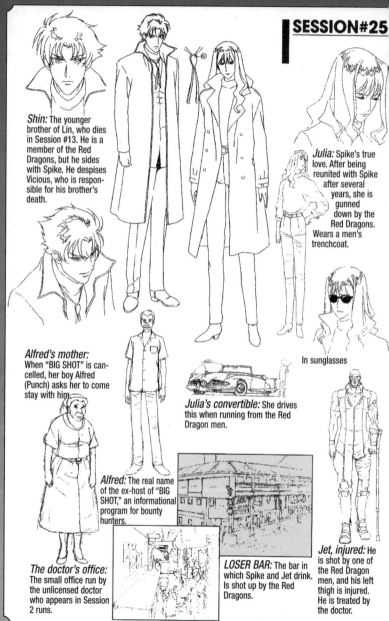

Shin: The younger brother of Lin, who dies in Session #13. He is a member of the Red Dragons, but he sides with Spike. He despises Vicious, who is responsible for his brother's death.

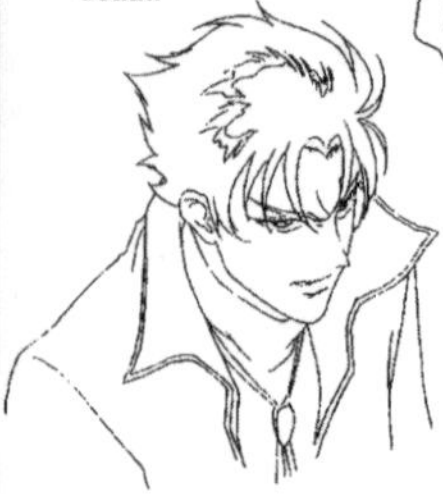

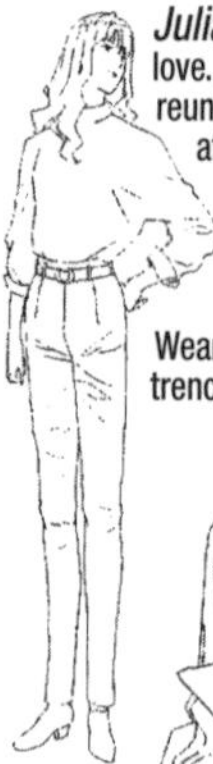

Julia: Spike's true love. After being reunited with Spike after several years, she is gunned down by the Red Dragons. Wears a men's trenchcoat.

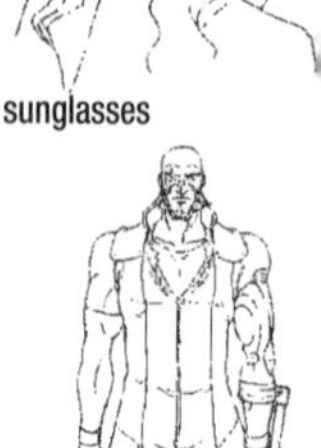

In sunglasses

Alfred's mother: When "BIG SHOT" is cancelled, her boy Alfred (Punch) asks her to come stay with him.

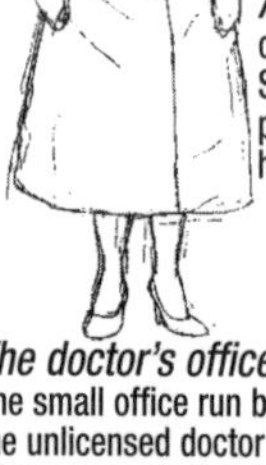

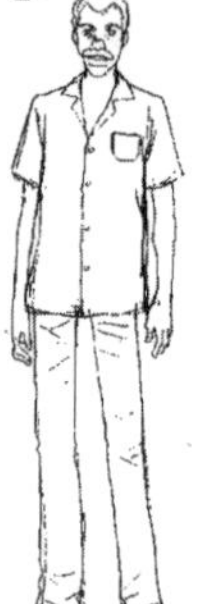

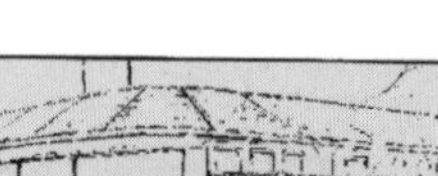

Julia's convertible: She drives this when running from the Red Dragon men.

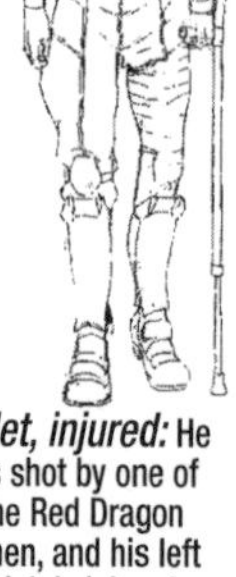

Alfred: The real name of the ex-host of "BIG SHOT," an informational program for bounty hunters.

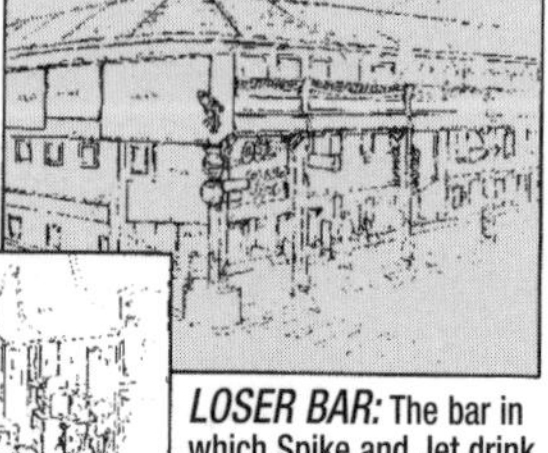

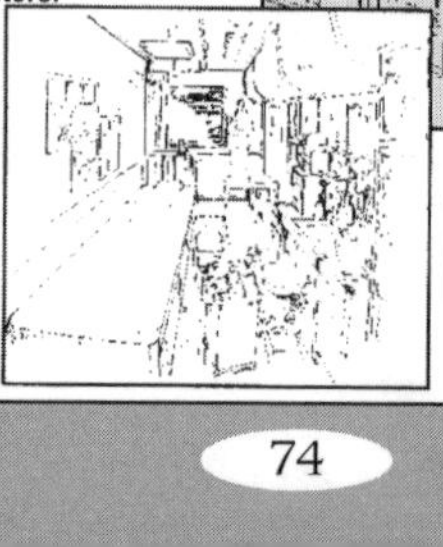

The doctor's office: The small office run by the unlicensed doctor who appears in Session 2 runs.

LOSER BAR: The bar in which Spike and Jet drink. Is shot up by the Red Dragons.

Jet, injured: He is shot by one of the Red Dragon men, and his left thigh is injured. He is treated by the doctor.

Vicious' subordinates: Attack the elders' chamber with Vicious in the beginning of Session 25.

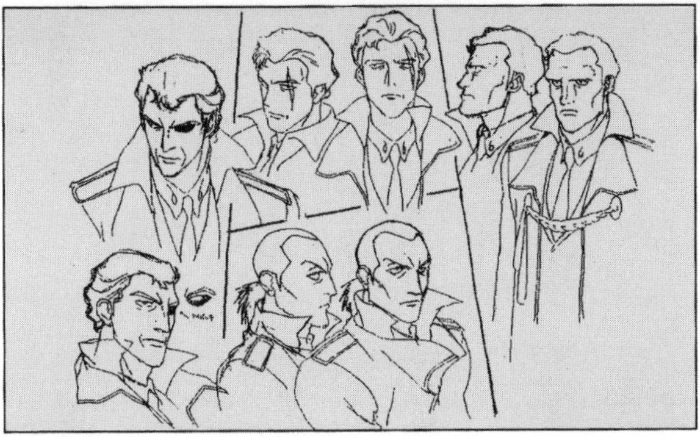

***The elders' subordinates* (2):** The four men who handle Vicious' punishment.

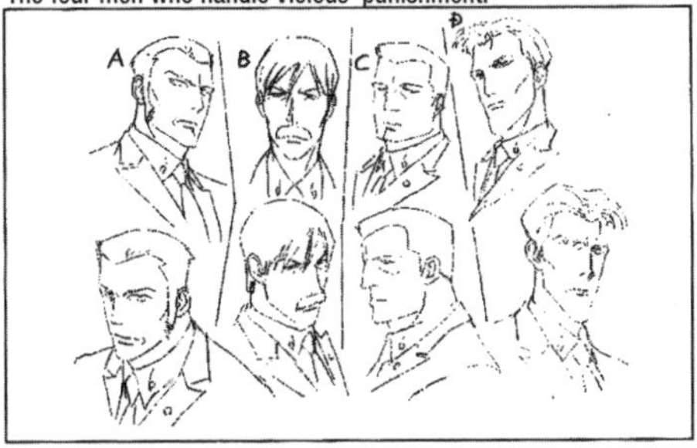
A
B
C
D

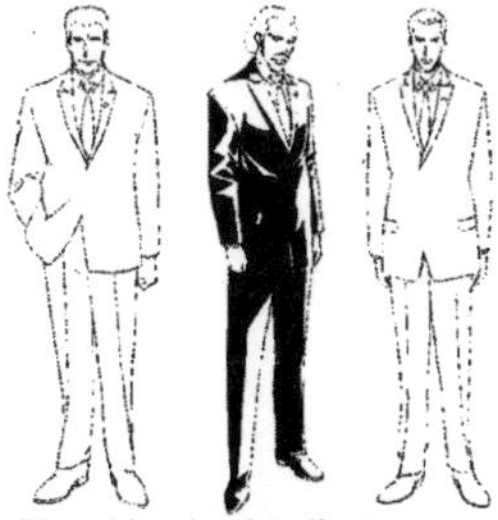

***The elders' subordinates* (1):** Red Dragon subordinates on the elders' side.

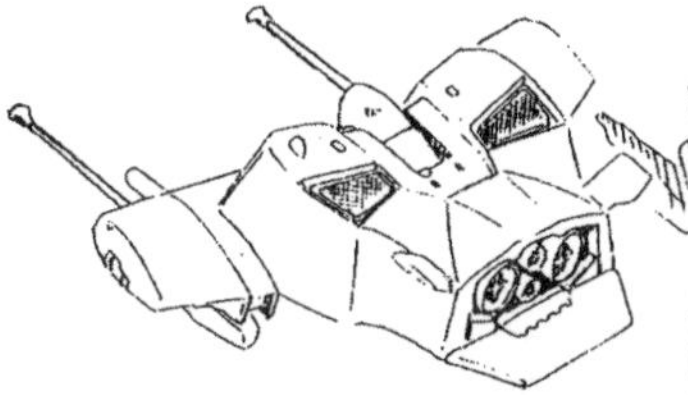

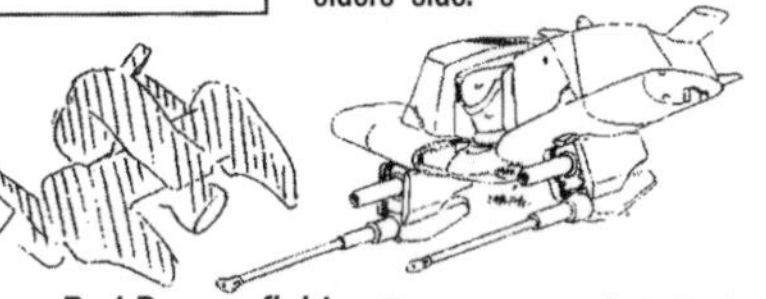

Red Dragon fighter: The monoarmor that attacks the Bebop. Has a lot of fighting power, but it doesn't have much maneuverability. Armed with a 35 mm cannon and two missile launchers.

The elders' room: The elders' chamber. The subordinates lie in wait on the stairs and on the upper corridors.

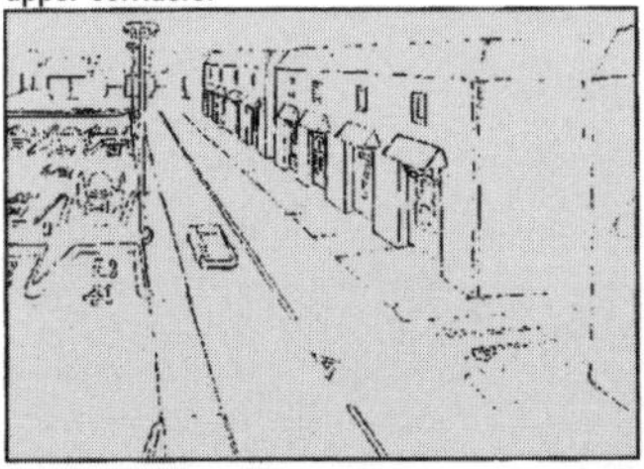

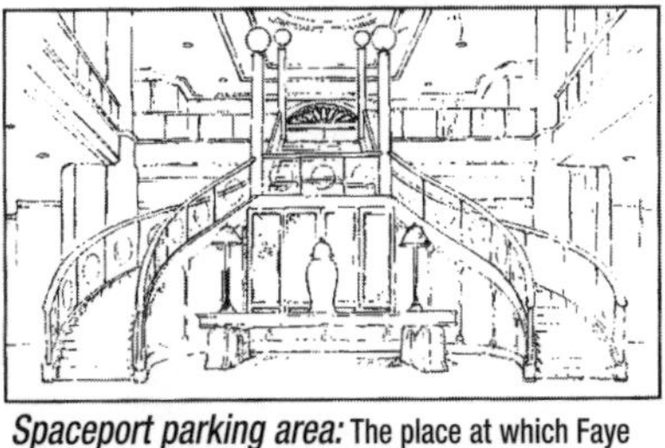

Spaceport parking area: The place at which Faye parks the Redtail. Faye and Julia met on the road alongside the parking area.

SESSION#26

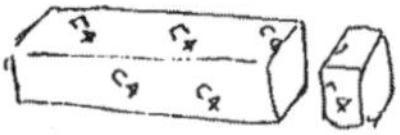
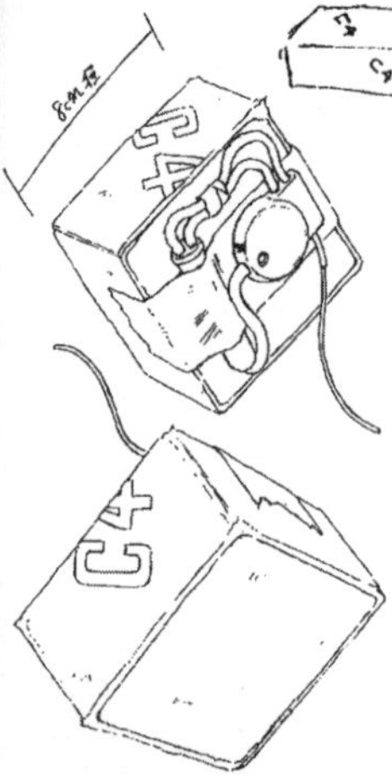
C4

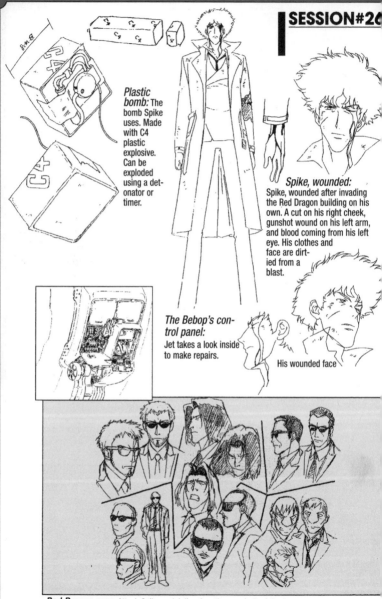

Plastic bomb: The bomb Spike uses. Made with C4 plastic explosive. Can be exploded using a detonator or timer.

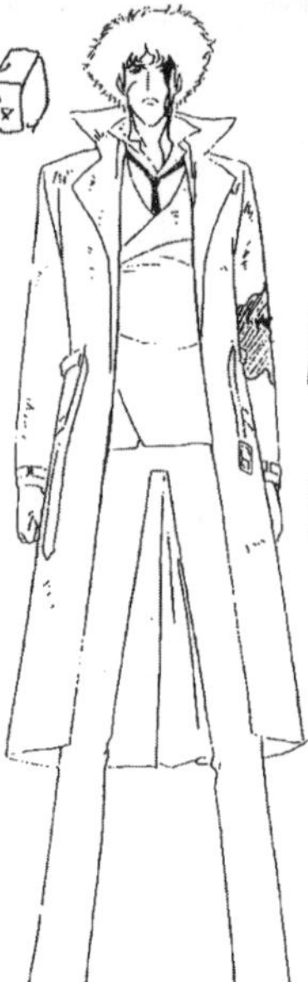

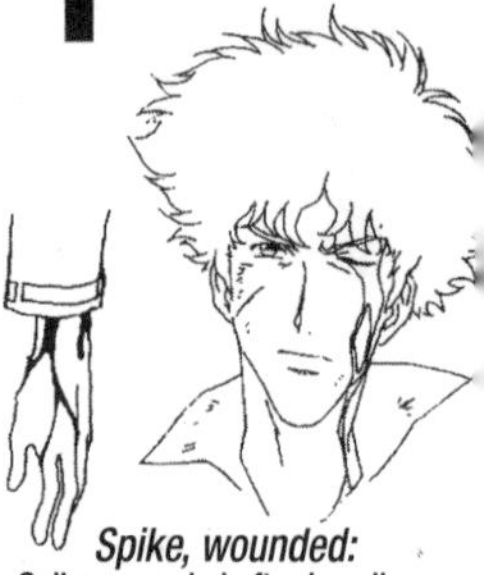

Spike, wounded: Spike, wounded after invading the Red Dragon building on his own. A cut on his right cheek, gunshot wound on his left arm, and blood coming from his left eye. His clothes and face are dirtied from a blast.

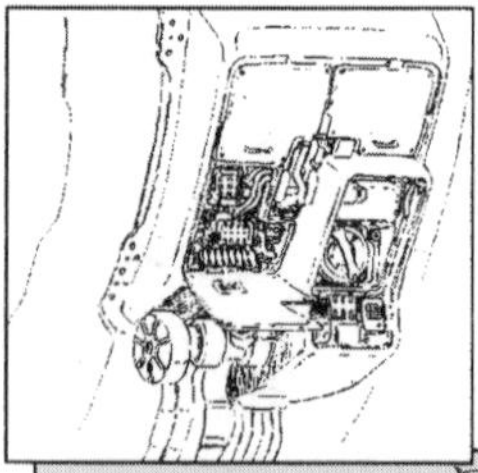

The Bebop's control panel: Jet takes a look inside to make repairs.

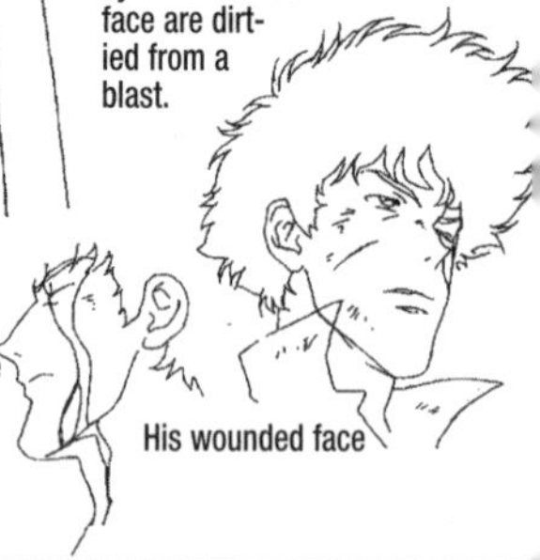

His wounded face

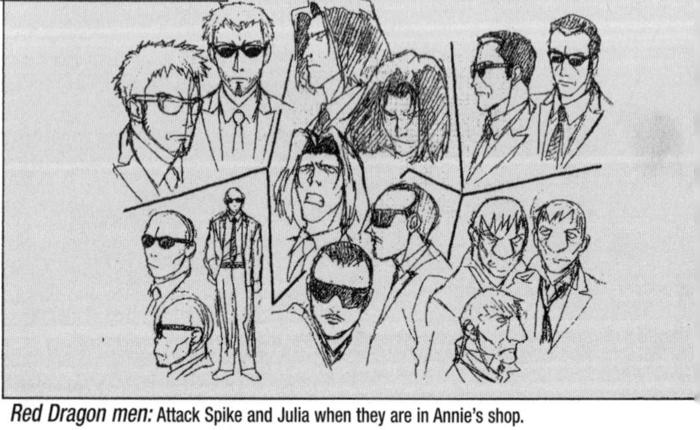

Red Dragon men: Attack Spike and Julia when they are in Annie's shop.

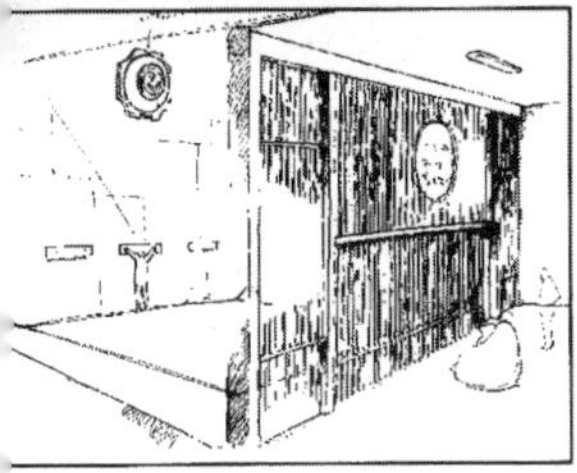

Judgment Room: The room where Vicious' punishment is to be carried out.

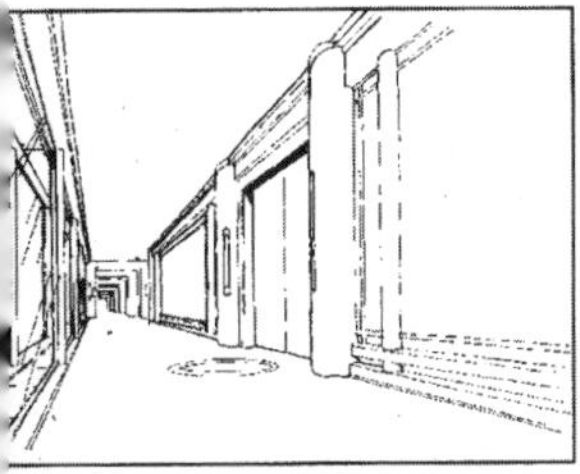

An inner corridor: Spike runs through here as bullets come pouring in from the glass window on the right.

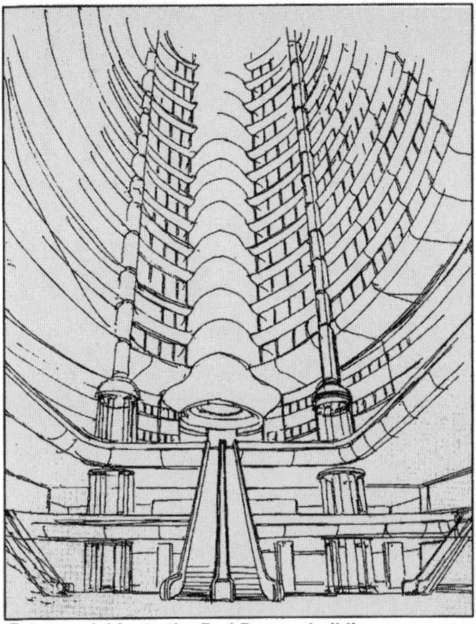

Entrance lobby to the Red Dragon building: Features high stairwells and a luxurious style which uses glass. The interior design has a blending of Japanese and Western elements.

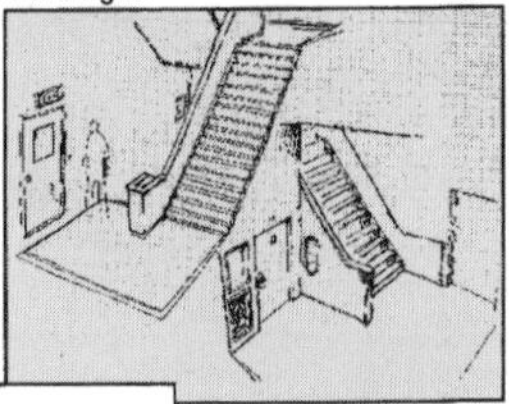

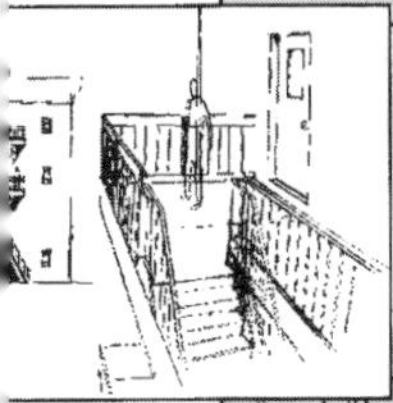

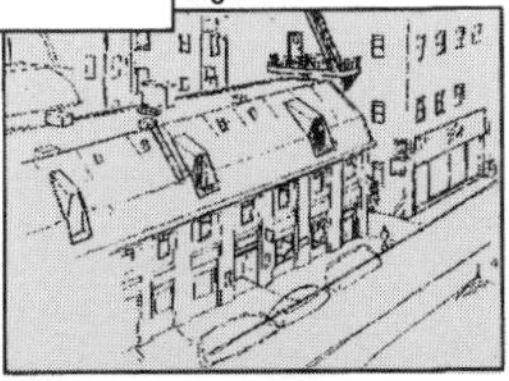

Inside Annie's shop, and the building next door:
Spike and Julia pass through here running away from their pursuers. Julia is shot on the building below.

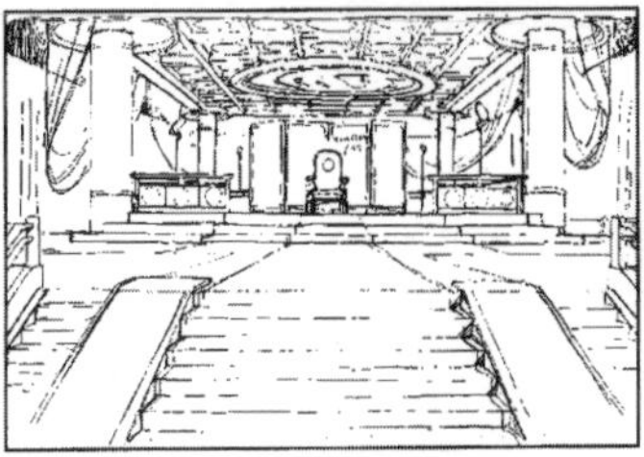

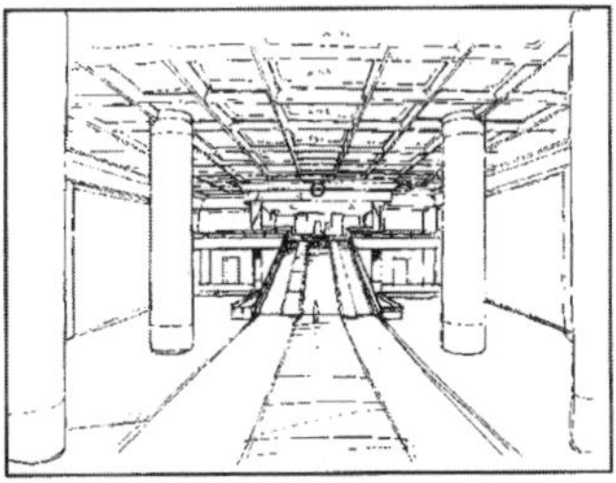

Ceremony room: The top floor in the Red Dragon building. The bottom picture is a view from the entry elevator

SEE YOU, SPACE COWBOY ...

Translator — Amy Forsyth
Retouch Artist — Eric Pineda
Cover Designer — Thea Willis
Graphic Designer — Anna Kernbaum

Senior Editor — Luis Reyes
Production Manager — Mario M. Rodriguez
Art Director — Matt Alford
VP of Production — Ron Klamert
Brand Manager — Kenneth Lee
Publisher — Stuart Levy

Email: editor@TOKYOPOP.com
Come visit us online at www.TOKYOPOP.com

A  book

TOKYOPOP® is an imprint of Mixx Entertainment, Inc. 5900 Wilshire Blvd.,
Ste. 2000, Los Angeles, CA 90036

ISBN: 1-59182-023-5

First TOKYOPOP® printing: September 2002

10 9 8 7 6 5 4 3 2 1
Printed in the USA